CHILD OF THE TWENTIES

FRANCES DONALDSON

Child of the Twenties

WEIDENFELD AND NICOLSON
LONDON

Published in Great Britain in 1986
by George Weidenfeld & Nicolson Limited
91 Clapham High Street
London SW4 7TA

ISBN 0 297 78888 4

Printed in Great Britain by
Redwood Burn Limited, Trowbridge, Wiltshire.

Foreword to the New Edition

P.G. Wodehouse always got much pleasure from reading his own novels. "I am reduced to English mystery stories and my own stuff," he wrote towards the end of his life. "I was reading *Blandings Castle* again yesterday and was lost in admiration for the brilliance of the writer."

I have none of this feeling for "my own stuff", and the last time I read *Child of the Twenties* was when I corrected the proofs.

Re-reading it more than twenty-five years later, I have been taken by surprise, both by the personality of the writer, a woman of fifty-two, and by that of the person she is writing about from childhood until the age of thirty-two. Both are subtly different from anyone I know now.

In the first place the sense of deprivation of everything which might be called culture is something I have forgotten. I have still not much feeling for the pictorial arts, but twenty-five years of accompanying my husband (for long a director of Covent Garden Opera House and of the English National Opera Company at the Coliseum) often three times a week to the opera or the theatre, and the society of many of the people who have since become my friends have, to some extent, appeased this feeling. Then I am taken aback by the rather acidulated tone in which I often refer to my mother, whom I now remember as someone I loved.

The picture of life immediately after the war would seem to me somewhat exaggerated but for two things. Somewhere in this book I remark "I am very truthful. I cannot help it." This is correct and makes me (except under the heaviest vows) a dangerous confidante, because I cannot help establishing what I believe to be the truth. Nor can I ever sleep peacefully if I have doubts about something I have written. So, personally I believe that the picture I have given is accurate within the bounds of skill. Secondly, when it was first published many people of my own age read the book and no one ever suggested it was untrue or exaggerated.

Rupert Hart-Davis published *Child of the Twenties* and when he first read it he said: "I like the second part the best. It has more feeling and it is feeling which makes a book." Re-reading it, I find myself agreeing with him. The first half is a description of my youthful surroundings and the world in which I grew up, and may today be the more interesting for that reason. The second is more personal.

Both parts show a picture of the life of the reasonably well-off before 1939 – before cooking, child-minding and washing-up took over, before the permissive society, and when no great loss of virtue attached to idleness.

FRANCES DONALDSON
London, 1986

1

IN my youth we had a book which was intended as a short cut to the analysis of personality. First came a list of questions that had to be answered Yes or No, and there was a method of marking the answers. The rest of the book contained the results of the different combinations, each an analysis of character. For a short time we used regularly to play this game with our friends.

It always seemed to me there was one key question, and that the die was cast by the answer to it, no matter what the combination of answers to the rest might be. That question was: Was your childhood happy? If the answer was Yes, one might discover one had all sorts of virtues and abilities, pleasant and likeable characteristics, but they would always be of a humdrum kind. A happy childhood, it seemed, disposed once and for all of any chance of spirituality, imaginativeness or brilliance.

This always distressed me, because by no distortion of self-pity could I claim an unhappy childhood. Possibly I should not so much have minded the dull character-readings my answers always produced if they had not confirmed my own impressions. The truth is I was conscious of a little commonplaceness. Yet I could not help regarding this detestable happy childhood as very bad luck, for from the smattering of the works of the followers of Freud I had by now acquired there seemed to have been so many influences that might have made it unhappy.

In the first place my parents were not in the least well suited. This fact became obvious, however, only much later in their lives, and during my childhood was submerged by their youth, their affectionate natures, by poverty and the struggle they had to keep alive, but most of all, I believe, because they had three children and a quite extraordinarily, in relation to their other characteristics, strong sense of family ties and their duty to them.

My father, Frederick Lonsdale, whom I have described at length elsewhere, was a very unusual man, a man of talent and wit and charm, but with the temperament of a genius. He was as instinctive and unpretentious as an animal, responding with a nervous exclusiveness to the demands of his own nature, and with as much sensitivity to the rules of human intercourse as a well trained cat. If one says that he was selfish and egotistical, that merely touches the edge of his exceptional self-centredness, which was in no way mean or introvert, but of an inspirational kind. He was almost impossible to live with, and, during the last thirty years of his life, he recognised this fact so well that he wandered aimlessly and alone round the world, avoiding any regularised human intimacy. In theory one might have counted on him to produce unhappy children.

He did produce a deep and continuing uneasiness. He was entirely capricious; good-tempered and gay, bad-tempered and viciously cruel, easily pleased and quick to praise, impossibly impatient and critical. His unchallengeable opinions were formed in a mind both shallow and uninformed, but his wits were of a very high order, his personal charm irresistible, and his personality was so strong that he imposed himself on everyone who came in contact with him. He had, both when he wished to please and when he wished to domineer, the rare and overwhelming gift of complete unexpectedness.

He taught us, my two sisters and myself, to be wary in human relations and to distrust the past. Nothing with him could be taken for granted or based on the ordinary presumption of previous experience. To this day I am always made nervous by people who have aroused my interest by seeming to like me; I cannot believe they will do so twice. So often we would go trustfully forward with some gesture of affection or some little joke which yesterday had warmed the day, only for this same thing to be the cause today of disastrous humiliation. One never opened the door of a room he was in, without pausing on the threshold to sense the atmosphere.

Second only to his capriciousness, his impatience had the most

10

lasting effects. He was so unreasonably easily bored. It seemed to us then that the test of the worth of anything was how it might strike him in his mood of the moment; but I wonder now did he aspire to teach us some of his own quick turn of speech? In any case, we learned that it was unpardonable to be dull for the shortest space of time, even in recounting the most necessary facts, and that we must constantly strain our wits and our senses to avoid it. But we had no wits and absolutely no idea of what he might find dull or amusing (he often surprised us by roaring with laughter and approval at some remark this particular sense of which we had been too slow to catch) and, if any of us have even the smallest hereditary share of his originality, he delayed its expression for years. We acquired at this time certain nervous tricks in conversation, interrupting ourselves constantly with "Do you want to hear all this?" or "Am I boring you?" and we always had one eye cocked on anyone who asked us a question needing time or thought, to see if he had really expected an answer.

"Don't keep finishing your sentences," he said to me once when I was telling him something; "I'm not a bloody fool."

He terrified us too with the expectations he had of us. In a restaurant he would pick out some famous figure of the day, Mr Gerald du Maurier or Mr Seymour Hicks, or Mr Arnold Bennett, sitting on the other side of the room. Selecting one of us he would tell her to cross the room and speak to the great man, and he would explain to her what she was to say. This would not be in the form of a message from himself, which might have been a possibility, but of a speech, which we could barely comprehend and could not conceivably have thought of, to be delivered as if an impulse of affection and wit had brought the chosen one across the room, alone and unprompted, to deliver it.

He rarely succeeded in this endeavour. Neglecting instantly the ginger-beer and delicious rolls that we had been consuming, we formed a rank of stubborn, embarrassed refusers. Just occasionally, however, he could, by flattery and cajolery, induce me to undertake the task. I was his favourite and would go to

11

great lengths to retain the position. But I always made a mess of this assignment, and would swiftly return, followed most likely by the great man himself, cigar in hand, come to find out what was behind the garbled words which, appearing from nowhere, I had suddenly thrown at him. Either way my father would say we were poops.

"It's so absurd," he would complain, "to be shy of So-and-So. He's a delightful fellow, and it would have amused him."

We did not much mind being called poops, and, once the incident was over, we returned quite happily to our ginger-beer. We knew it was a far, far better thing to be a poop than to have the kind of temperament that could have carried off his mission with verve and spontaneity. To be a poop was a pity and very disappointing for him, but to be a show-off was to invite the cutting edge of a tongue that, in its day, was feared all over London.

It was a curious feature of my childhood, the horror all grown-ups had of showing off, a horror equally strong in all the other families I knew. It was terribly difficult not to show off, because there seemed to be no clear understanding in anyone's mind of what this was. Roughly it applied to any spontaneous effort at self-expression that did not quite come off, as well as to all attempts to draw attention to oneself. Nowadays, when children play for attention, their parents suffer greatly but in silence, because they know that in some way they have failed to provide a proper environment for the developing nature, lacked something in love or in their main duty to induce a sense of security, and that it is this which has made the poor little thing behave in this excruciatingly shaming way. They know, too, that it is no use now attempting to fill this gap with admonition, because, to a child seeking attention, any response will do and will encourage repetition of his unpleasing performance. So, humble and flinching, they bear it. But in my childhood our parents were unaware of these basic facts and free to give rein to their inclinations. Showing off they regarded as the very devil, to be flattened out of their children no matter what the pain inflicted. All attempts at candour, friendliness, gaiety or wit could come under

12

the heading, as well as boasting or affectation. To a childish mind it is impossible to draw the delicate line between the effusions of spirit likely to be successful and showing off, and so, as one of my contemporaries remarked, we spent the whole of our childhood learning to be incapable of all the things that would be considered most delightful once we were grown up. I think this accounts for the arrogance of manner which was a marked attribute of my generation in our early youth. The sudden demand to behave in a way we had been taught was insufferable was too much for us, and we took refuge in superciliousness.

My father was very hot against showing off. Apart from the fact that it bored and irritated him in a way he could not bear, he had a strong and puritan sense of his duty to teach us not to be in the least like himself.

But, although he was a natural scourge to the young, reducing the whole of life at a superficial level to a nerve-racking obstacle-race, he loved us, and he adopted quite naturally the role of the responsible family man. It is curious the enormous importance this had. We loved him devotedly in return and were never in the least unhappy. We regarded him in his worst moods only as an uncomfortable wind that raged up suddenly on calm and happy days, or as the maddening little breeze that blows in the garden, fluttering the papers one is trying to read, and we minded him no more than that other rough wind that blustered off the east-coast shore onto our youthful cheeks. We were always conscious too that he was very unusual, and we would have put up with a great deal more for the pride it gave us that he was not as other men.

Nevertheless, when I look back to these days, I simply marvel at him. It seems to me so very surprising that, with his intense moodiness, and the huge egotism that propelled him through the world and later was to waste away his talents and destroy his natural zest for life, that with a pathological desire for independence which forced him to break with every other tie, he should have had this one inescapable instinct that bound him to his family.

My mother was the only woman to whom, in his fashion, he was permanently faithful. When they were old they could never meet, because they could not be in a room together for ten minutes without falling into a screaming tempestuous quarrel which made them ill and left them with days of bitter reflection before them until their emotion subsided. Yet one never ceased to feel they loved each other. He always wrote to her regularly, and, if anything went wrong, he assumed without question his duty to put it right. If she was ill he went into a stiff-faced panic. Of course he always felt guilty towards her, but, in most people, guilt serves only the purposes of original sin, holding the door against joy, tingeing like whisky the hues of the morning, supine and uninspired. In my father it preserved him from triviality.

But in the days of which I speak, I think he simply loved her, and she loved him and us, and stood bravely between us and the worst of his vagaries, a jolly, healthy girl, with nerves strong enough to stand his temperament, and I think they enjoyed life.

Before I can speak of my mother, I must record the other circumstance of my childhood I find rather tiresome. It was middle-class. It is not that I have found it such a handicap to come from the middle classes, but simply that there are no advantages. The upper classes have enormous advantages in every sphere of life, and this is so even if one wishes to be a writer. My contemporaries and older people have begun to write their autobiographies, and I find it extraordinary how many of them come from an upper-class background. This is inestimable when it comes to material for memoirs.

In childhood there are the splendid old nannies who have been for years in the family and have the valuable gift of treating every-one as if he was a child; there are the dour Scotch gardeners, and the stables where the ponies stand, which the writer was often too sensitive to ride. Usually there are woods and a gamekeeper, at the very worst some curious hut in the laurel bushes, a perfect object for fantasy. Above all there are the eccentric uncles and aunts and the hordes of cousins and connections. The upper classes had this enormous propensity for intermarriage which

14

produced a wealth of background material, in that it related the whole group through and through. It is sometimes thought that in England they renewed themselves by their willingness to marry outside their own class, but this is not strictly true. It was done far more by their ready acceptance of the sons of the newly rich, and, while the males of the older families did occasionally marry beneath them, this was usually for money, or from the perfect sensuality that can be satisfied only by chorus girls, and both these things made for delicious eccentricity in uncles and aunts.

Then there are the private schools, and Eton and Balliol, and some great regiment, all the glamorous contemporaries who, having since made a name for themselves, cannot fail to be interesting in even the smallest details of their childhood. If the worst comes to the worst, there are all the other writers, for in the early years of the century upper-class literary people naturally herded together. In turn, it is possible for all the children of all these people to present, skilfully and with the candour only permitted to the artist, accounts of all the little squabbles and all the little family jokes they shared between them.

"I will not write about my contemporaries," Hilaire Belloc said, "for fear of offending them." Nowadays, fortunately for us, the friends of poets are made of stronger stuff.

However, everyone who wishes to write memoirs cannot be of the upper class, and the next best thing today is to come from the working class. Before the last war George Orwell wrote a book in which he said there was an impassable barrier between the upper and middle and the lower classes, because the lower classes smelled. In a contortion of apology and disassociation, Mr Gollancz wrote a foreword saying that Orwell had said "In the opinion of the middle class in general, the working class smells." But this, as I understand it, is not true. Orwell did not say that in the opinion of the middle class in general the working class smelled; he said they smelled. In any case, it is not really of any importance, because there is no doubt they did smell.

Curiously enough, it is just these smells that pay off so well nowadays in a working-class autobiography. The ripe smell of fresh sweat on the men, the sour smell of stale sweat on the women, the smell of cabbages cooking, or of the weekly wash boiling, the suffocating smell of working-class mother-love, the ammonia in the communal lavatory, the smell of sickly children and inadequate drains. . . . to my middle-class nose these smells are all strictly revolting either in life or on the printed page; but the book-critics are avid for them. Any writer who can reproduce them is certain of a column to himself in both the Sunday papers, followed by eulogies in the weeklies, and when Christmas comes he can be confident of finding his book amongst the best of the year. I am not sure why the critics find these smells so appealing. Maybe they keep them in vicarious touch with life; or maybe they plump the vanity, reminding them that it is all a question of talent, to each his own. Some have old nannies, eccentric uncles, famous friends; for all the rest there are smells.

But the one thing that no one is anxious to hear about is the life of the middle classes. The middle classes are inhibited, sterile, pretentious and mainly philistine. They are without charm, originality or courage. They produce the dullest women in the world, and no natural background for autobiography.

This may be taken for overstatement. Before the last war the middle class also had servants. But the fact is that these were never eccentric. The middle classes had not the confidence. It took a member of the upper class to say to her guests: "There is absolutely nothing to show you in the garden. Smith has pruned the roses to death, and he has the opposite of green fingers. Unfortunately he's been with us for years, and his father was here before him."

No middle-class woman could have said that. In the first place it was unlikely to be true; in the second, if by some unusual chance it had been, it would have been regarded as a grave piece of affectation. In my youth it might, in fact, have been possible for an acute observer to place the social position of almost anyone by his attitude to his servants. If someone remarked of his butler: "You'd better watch out when he takes the food round. He's always been a perfect clown, and now he's going blind as well," you could be absolutely certain you were in the presence of a hereditary social position. Nowadays, of course, it would only mean that you had better watch out when he took the food round. This will be a great loss to the future writers of memoirs. It is not so much that the "dailies" of today are quite without their eccentricities, as that they become funny only if the full distinction between their place in society and that of their employers can be carefully drawn beforehand.

In my family the servants were not eccentric because my mother engaged them, but I have to admit that my father could always be trusted to be fairly eccentric in his behaviour towards them. He kept an only moderately competent manservant for several years because, having been in the Air Force during the first war, he made it possible for my father, when actors who came to dinner had retained their wartime rank for social purposes, to say to him: "Leading Aircraftman Hichens, bring Major So-and-So some brandy."

But my father was a very odd man, and he is of importance here only because by his oddities he broke up the pattern, and also because, later in life, he succeeded in hauling me after him to a position whence it was possible to see more than one aspect; but he was not the strongest influence in my environment.

And, if the middle classes are dull, they are always with us. They are one of the two great interweaving strands that make up the English character; beside them the upper class is just a small coterie with an esoteric language and views on their own superiority for which, except in relation to their opportunities, there are absolutely no grounds. So it is just to the extent that my childhood was middle-class that it interests me now. The world of the autobiographies I read, the world where the arts are taken for granted, and intellectual pursuits and attainments a common heritage, and where the countryside and countrymen form a background to a life in which a sense of privilege and leisure contribute so effectively to an innocent assumption of natural ability, was not my world. And the rich texture of experience that emerges from the pages of these writers is as foreign to me as if I had lived in a different country in another century, or on the other side of George Orwell's impassable barrier.

As I go through life I often feel like a person wandering about in a picture gallery, looking at the pictures—liking some, disliking others, with little taste and without either knowledge or judgment. And I think then that, if there had been someone at my elbow to guide me, who had explained to me what the painters were trying to do and where they had succeeded, in what way they derived from their tremendous past, and when they were merely experimenting, then, as we wandered round, he might have awakened my interest, and I, too, might have been able to see the pictures instead of just looking at them. And so, I think, must many of my contemporaries feel.

2

MY father married my mother because she was the prize. If his vision of the world had been a larger one, or his social position nearer hers, he might not have done so.

He was the son of a tobacconist in the town of St Helier in Jersey. He was born, I believe, in a two-roomed cottage somewhere on the sea front, and his father remained there all his life, a small tradesman. My father was wild and unmanageable in his youth, and, by a system of inveterate truancy and by firmly closing his mind, he managed to evade even the moderate education he might normally have acquired. But he was spontaneously talented in the inexplicable way of an infant prodigy, and, while he was still very young, he had his first play produced, and, acquiring in this way what seemed to him a considerable sum of money, he returned to the town of his birth to show himself off. While he was there his eye lighted on the belle of the island.

My mother lived also in St Helier as a child, but her father was a retired Colonel of the Royal Artillery and a partner in a cramming school which prepared young men for the Army. He bought his tobacco from my paternal grandfather. Somewhere behind these two families there must have been a small and select group of people whom neither of them met, the Lieutenant Governor of the island and the families of the local aristocrats, the latter descended from the Normans. But if I am right, it was not apparent to my father's eyes, and not admitted in the sense I have suggested by my mother's family.

This family placed, or so it has always seemed to me, a weight even for those days quite out of proportion to reality or good sense upon their social position. My grandfather, always a poor man, was forced all his life as a soldier to take advantage of a system then existing in the Army, which allowed richer men to trade with him their turn for service in those parts of the Empire where life could be lived comparatively cheaply, in return for his in England. He spent all his time abroad, and when he rose to command his regiment and my grandmother might have enjoyed the pleasures of Colonel's lady, her health prevented it and they were forced to retire to Jersey. Here they inhabited a house which, when I visited it several years ago in search of the facts of my father's early life, amazed me by its small size and dreary appearance—a house in a row of other houses such as might be seen in any of the poorer streets in any seaside town in England.

Perhaps these facts combined in my grandfather's mind to make him stand so strongly on what he believed unassailable— his position as a gentleman. In any case, stand he did, and so stood his whole family with him, not merely referring all questions constantly and openly to how in their social position they should behave, nor simply relating everything to this touchstone of superiority, but seemingly imposing their own view of themselves on everyone who came in contact with them. Or perhaps I exaggerate. Certainly in the view from the tobacconist's door their social standing bulked very large, and equally certainly my mother kept this picture of her high birth steadily in front of my father's youthful eyes (although to do both of them justice it was never a source of contention between them, nor a matter which, in their regard, weighed the balance against his talents, but simply a fact, a pleasant and undeniable fact) and taught her children to believe in it.

My mother must have been a very pretty girl. She had strongly curling auburn hair (although it turned grey so early that I never saw it so), a good skin, a clear complexion and a good figure. My father, lounging about the streets of the town, having only partially succeeded in his desire to impress the inhabitants, made up his mind to marry her. If there had been on the scene some greater prize, some bigger challenge to his effrontery, all our history might have been different, because, at this time in his life, he combined with his ineluctable charm so much faith in his powersthat I cannot imagine how anyone could have resisted him.

At the same time he could never have succeeded so easily with my mother had it not been for the skill with which he imposed himself on my grandmother, who seems to have fallen in love with him, as women sometimes do with their daughters' lovers. In any case, she intrigued for him and lied to my grandfather, encouraged my mother to a course which, left to herself, she would have viewed as, owing to the class-difference, impossible, and finally sped them on their romantic elopement.

After this they starved on and off for several years, and gave birth to three daughters, of which I was the second. During the whole of my childhood our family fortunes were highly unstable, varying from easily earned riches, quickly spent, to a disconcerting feeling of worry about money, but, from the time I was old enough to remember anything, my father was an established playwright, and the extreme and romantic poverty of my parents' youth a thing of the past. We lived always in some quite respectable, undistinguished little house (frequently changed), and we had servants of a sort, and a series of young, untrained girls who acted as nanny and whom we called by their christian names. My parents had made friends with the doctor and his wife, the schoolmaster and his wife, and our world had assumed a pattern it was to retain until I was grown up.

I wish that I knew what my mother was like then. In my mind there are two absolutely different people, the woman who was there when I was a child and the woman she afterwards grew into, and I have no idea whether the difference was in her or in myself. Certainly it seems impossible that the healthy, amiable, beneficently powerful young woman who was responsible for the happiness of my childhood could ever have grown into the older woman, but equally, when I regard the recollections I have of that time, both in the light of my knowledge of her later character and of my adult understanding, I can recall only one incident that suggests the temperament that was later to be so pronounced and so insanely provoking, and that is a very small thing, which could easily be explained in other ways.

If one has a very great physical need of someone, this has a transfiguring power, as I suppose is known to everyone who has ever fallen out of love or suffered pain. And the physical needs of children who do not live in a suite of nursery rooms under the care of nannies and nursery-maids, but have only a young girl called Mabel to look after them, pump blood to the severed natal cord long after in the children of grander households it may have withered away. We did not meet our parents only in the evenings and after we had changed our clothes, but shared the whole of life with them, and this was true from the earliest age that I can remember. And, except for her name, I cannot remember Mabel at all, because in moments of stress, the high points of recollection, it was my mother who came to my aid.

I think she was physically exceptionally comforting. She was always very natural in her ways and had no inhibitions either about demonstrations of affection or about the more sordid side of family care. Personally I have always cleared up after my children when they were sick, and changed their nappies when they were babies, but I have never especially cared for it, and my nostrils have an unfortunate tendency to curl away from these jobs. I do not think my mother had any feeling about them at all, any more than she ever had any particular reticence about any of the natural functions, discoursing to us from the earliest age on every possible subject, including her own attitude to physical love.

Certainly it is in moments of pain or physical discomfort that I remember her best, and it was these that returned to me at the end to revive in unexpected sorrow and uneasiness the tie which, unsuspected, had held throughout the years. When I was a child and my pillow hot, my undersheet a corrugated trap for wakefulness, she only had to walk into the room to bring peace with her; and when I was in bed with some small illness, if she plumped the pillows behind my head I lay so happily reading my book against the cool luxury of the linen that, for years, until after I was married, I regarded the annual return of 'flu as one of the pleasant things to look forward to. In our family, when we had starved for two or three days and the fever was gone, we

22

were always brought for breakfast on the first day of returned and ravenous appetite a concoction called egg-in-a-cup. This consisted of a piece of buttered toast cut into small shapes like *croûtons* with a softly boiled egg broken over it and plenty of pepper and salt. Every illness seemed well worth it for the moment when, sitting up in bed in a flannel dressing gown, one's hair tied severely back after a hot bath, one waited for this.

I think she had a feeling for bed herself which led her to make it so delightful for other people. Every so often she used to take a day in bed, for no particular reason except that she found it replenishing, and then she too would have the best and cleanest linen, and trays of food brought up to her, and we would sit in her room and talk to her, and it was then, as well as every day when she was in the bath, that she began to make us at the earliest age her confidantes in all her most intimate affairs.

The only incident of my childhood in which I felt she had failed me occurred when I was ill in bed. I had been there for several days and was getting better, and she sat on my bed in the evening playing with me. I have forgotten exactly what happened, but I must have said I would bite her, because I remember her sitting on the bed, smiling at me and playfully daring me to do this. Then I remember biting her quite hard on the knuckles of her hand. Instantly the scene changed and she stood up, stiffly angry and reproachful. I could have borne the anger, for this is an everyday matter in childhood, but I hotly resented the reproaches. She said that I was an impossible child, hard and self-centred and without gratitude (children in those days were expected to be constantly and consciously grateful), and then she left the room. Outside I heard her tell my father who was come to say good-night to me not to come into my room. "She has been very naughty indeed and she had better be left alone."

For hours I waited alone in bed, but, late at night, after she had finished dinner, she came back to see if I was still awake.

"Are you sorry?" she asked me, and behind her manner, which was still stiff and formal, I saw that there was a softening. She

23

wanted me to be sorry. I was sorry, and I said so willingly, sorry that there should be this breach between us, sorry that my father had not come to say good-night, sick of lying in coventry alone in the dark. But, although I did not say this, I was not sorry that I had bitten her, for I still felt convinced that there had been an agreement between us that I should do so.

I know now that I was not wrong, that what happened was that I bit too hard, and, when I suddenly hurt her, she lost her temper, and, since she did not feel inclined to admit this, she had to pretend it was my behaviour that was at fault. And later on this was to become a repetitive pattern. First the unexpected small quarrel, then no opportunity to explain one's part, but always the absolute necessity to apologise, with both my sisters saying: "Go on. You know you'll have to do it, so you may as well get it over." But I do not see this incident as necessarily reflecting the same implacable complacence. It is exceedingly difficult to apologise for losing one's temper with children, not merely because of the humiliation of suddenly having to come down to their level, but because of the shock and embarrassment it is apt to occasion them. Many women much wiser than my mother might have behaved as she did, in an effort not to chip at the child's feeling of security, without realising that this lies deeply embedded in truth. And the fact that I remember this incident with such clarity proves, I think, that it was of a kind most rare in my childhood. Would that, in the inconsequent but percipient recollections of one's own children, one could get away with so little.

In our household there were no smells. Although she never thought so, and I did not realise it then, there was something unusual in my mother's feeling for cleanliness. Every member of the family had two hot baths every day. Moving, as we did throughout my childhood, from one small and inconvenient house to another, I cannot imagine how she managed the hot water for all this bathing, but manage it she did, simply considering it, as we all learned to do, one of the necessities of life. Later on when we used to come back from school for the holidays, the first thing she did was to put us one after the other into the bath, washing our hair and our ears and our necks and cutting our nails. She believed that we had not been properly clean once in the whole three months we had been away. This constant immersion in hot water was to her not merely a duty but a pleasure, and so it is to me, an everlasting solace in times of cold, fatigue, illness, boredom or depression, a stimulus to reflection, a tranquilliser and a pick-me-up. Nowadays when, through the lack of servants or the shortage of coal, or when travelling, large quantities of hot water are sometimes difficult to achieve, I notice that many people are quite indifferent to the pleasures of the hot bath, even glad of an excuse to avoid it. This I cannot understand, because to me it seems impossible to live without.

There was a bottle of Sanitas, too, sold with a cork that, reversed, had a channel in it which in answer to a shake emitted a small spray of the disinfectant. My mother was always walking about the upstairs part of the house, waving this about.

Nearly all my memories of childhood are of sickness or of small unhappiness, I suppose because it passed so smoothly, without spur to the imagination or recollection. During my childhood we lived altogether in five different houses. The first was at Westgate, a small semi-detached house in a row. I remember little of it except that in our day-nursery we had a wallpaper with pictures of John Gilpin's ride. I remember, too, standing on a half-landing between two flights of stairs and for the first time feeling my heart ache. My mother, who was in her bedroom off the half-landing, said that she needed a stamp, and my elder sister said eagerly: "Oh! I've got one. I'll give it to you." Then she stumped up the top flight of stairs to the nursery and returned with her stamp. But it was a used one that she had licked off an incoming envelope. In these circumstances of disappointment I might, I suppose, have grieved for either my mother or my sister. But my heart belonged to my mother, and for her it ached. She had expected a proper stamp and had received this useless thing.

I have a vague memory, too, of being pushed out from this

25

house in the afternoons in a double pram with my sister. There was a dwarf who lived in Westgate, and wore dark clothes and a bowler hat. He was, I believe, an intelligent and gentle person, but our nursemaid managed to invest him with a pleasantly eerie quality. I think this nursemaid was Mabel, and I think she was adept at providing us with excitements. Later, in Birchington, we used on our walks to pass the house of a madwoman. It was known that she was mad, because she had pushed the end of her bed against the window of her room and slept with her feet stuck out of it in an effort to cool them. We never passed this window without looking up in terrified hope of a glimpse of those feet.

It must have been during a rich period that we first moved to Birchington, because we had a house there which stood in its own grounds, with two tennis courts. Once while we were there a great tennis-player called Wilding visited us and played on these courts. I remember his visit for two reasons. One, because my youngest sister, aged about three, shocked me so deeply by running out into the garden stark naked to see "the tennis man." The other, because Mr Wilding told my father that when he had first come to England and someone had said to him; "I hear you're a great tennis player," he had replied: "Well, I'm world champion, you know," but that now that he understood the English better, he smiled and replied to this remark: "Well, yes, I play a little." But it is surprising now to realise that I understood the implications of this story at that time, because I could not have been more than six; or did I, perhaps, only realise that both my father and Mr Wilding thought the English very silly, and, because of this, remember the details?

It was in this house, too, that a bird flew one day into the hall, and my mother had near-hysterics while my father tried to catch it, becoming responsible, or so I think, with this scene for the fact that I have an unreasonable feeling about birds to this day.

Later we moved to 6 Beach Avenue, the house that I remember best, and now we must have been poor again, because this was another semi-detached house in a row. It was opposite the public tennis courts and we used to climb over the wall when we wanted to play.

We were completely unimaginative children, never indulging in fantasy, and, I speak here for myself, without any interior life. But while we were at 6 Beach Avenue, the du Mauriers used to come down to Birchington, and then Daphne used to make us play Roundheads and Cavaliers in the shrubbery at the end of the tennis courts. It is the only imaginative game I ever remember playing, and I did not enjoy it.

It was early established that I was the sensible one. My elder sister was very nervous, and my younger chockful of oddities. It was thought that they had both inherited some of my father's temperament, but I was very stolid, could be relied on to tell the truth, and, except that I had a very hot temper, was quite exceptionally good. Perhaps that is why, on the only occasion I did show signs of peculiarity, my mother reacted with gratifying swiftness.

My sister had been ill and the doctor had recommended a change. She was sent, with me to keep her company, to recuperate with two maiden ladies who lived in a small farmhouse near Tenterden. They were not friends of my family, and I think must have been people who took paying guests to supplement a small income. My sister and I did not like it at all. The house was exceedingly cold and very bare, and, in the attic bedroom in which we slept, the beds were uncomfortable and not like the ones we were used to. Inside and outside the house there was absolutely nothing to do, although it was obviously felt, and this added shame to our discomfort, that with a farm all round us we ought to be able to amuse ourselves. The only vivid recollections I have of the place are of standing beside a small muck-heap in an orchard, shivering with cold and looking at my sister in absolute despair, and, on the same afternoon, of being taken to Tenterden where some embroidery was bought for us to do, of the kind that, after coarse orange flowers have been sewn on to it, is turned into a tray-cloth. That night my sister wept in bed, because she was homesick and unhappy, but I was visited by more hysterical feelings. The next day I wrote to my mother and told her that she must come at once and take us away. Although I do not remember this, I apparently suggested that it would be unnecessary to hurt the old ladies' feelings by telling them we did not like it, and that she must think of some better excuse. I do not remember the letter, although I do recall the feeling of guilt towards my hostesses which, after I had posted it, lessened the violence of my desire to get away; but there must have been extreme urgency in it, because, when my mother received it, she immediately hired a car, which she could not afford, and arrived to fetch us at the earliest possible moment of my expectations.

And, although this incident was not much noted at the time, it was later to become a known pattern of behaviour in my family, not of mine but of my father's. I have described elsewhere how, once he left our home, which he did in his early forties, he travelled incessantly about the world, seldom staying for more than a few days in any one place, spending on boats and trains an income that would have kept several families in luxury, impelled to be always on the move by a kind of cosmic claustrophobia; also of how, when late in his life he lived entirely in hotels, he required sums of money almost impossible for him to find, because he could endure life only in the Ritz-type of hotel. Usually these moves were made from boredom and from one familiar place, to which he would presently return, to another. But at other times, when he found the place he was in unsympathetic, and if anyone said one word against a place he had previously liked it immediately became unsympathetic, a little madness shone out of the sudden sharpness of his eyes and his unnaturally grim face. He drove everyone connected with him crazy with his eccentricities, but I could understand him a little because, in a small way, I know how he felt. There is a feeling of smear that comes over one, a very deep depression. The smear is both physical and of the soul. It is impossible to touch things, the furniture, or the pillow at night, and it is impossible to think of the people one loves because of the humiliating change in one-self, the fine coating of drab second-rateness all over one, which,

28

as if one suddenly found oneself shut up in a madhouse, must be fought off at once or may be with one forever. It has as much to do with boredom or inability to stand discomfort as people's dislike of spiders has to do with physical fear. It is in essence claustrophobic and is brought on by material things, oil-cloth, the smell of other people's soap, a certain kind of tawdry decoration, Victorian hangings. There were years when I could not sleep in a fourposter bed, because imprisoned in it with me were all the fug and dust and cobwebs of the years, all the bodies that had died in it, and the moth-balls of the living. When I was an adolescent and used to stay with school-friends, I often found their houses not what I had expected, and then I would always send myself telegrams, or, telephoning to my mother, conduct a one-sided conversation in which it was made plain to her and to my hosts that I was urgently needed at home.

But I grew out of all these things, and now only suffer as my father did, in second-class hotels, and even then I give in to it because on holidays the enormous guilt I feel about the money we are spending can be kept underground and prevented from ruining the whole thing only if I can manage to enjoy myself incessantly.

Once in Amiens we spent a long time looking for a certain small hotel where we had been told the food was good, and, when at last we arrived there, the steering of the car broke in front of the door of the hotel. Because of this, Jack went off to find a garage, leaving me to book a room and get the suitcases taken up. When I went into the bedroom there was a strong, close smell, and there were crimson hangings on the beds of a colour that has very fusty associations for me. I went down on to the pavement and marched up and down until Jack came back.

"What's the matter?" he asked me.

"We can't sleep there."

"Why not?"

"It's too long since the windows of the room were opened."

"All right," he said, and going up to the bedroom he dragged all the suitcases down again, and we went to the Grand Hotel.

On the same holiday we arrived in Troyes late at night and were shown into a bedroom where bright orange distemper was flaking off the walls.

I looked at Jack.

"I can't. . . ."

"All right," he said again, with a not unkind resignation, and we motored fifty miles to Chalons-sur-Saône which turned out to be worth it, because, although the bedroom was not very much better, the food was marvellous, and we talked for hours to the *patronne* about whether the chickens from Bresse were really the best, and if so why, and also about all the other restaurants we had visited on our holiday, each of which she knew either personally or by reputation. But Jack is only so amenable because it is a holiday, and because he also has the feeling of guilt about the money, and dare not risk it all being spoiled. And this is a difference between being a man and a woman. A man can always find women who are prepared to put up with this sort of thing, whereas a woman must learn to control it or to live alone.

There is little more I recall about my early childhood. Memory is a very inconsequent thing. I once heard P. G. Wodehouse say that almost the only thing he could remember learning in his schooldays was the riddle: What did the talkative negro say when he fell in a vat of boiling oil? and the answer, In-de-fat-i-gabble, and that this was not merely no use to him, but a positive nuisance. And in the same way I remember that, when my aunt came to stay and wore with her nightdress and dressing-gown a very pretty frilled cap, my father made no comment, but after going downstairs, added his bowler hat to his pyjamas. And I remember that, when we were very young and they did not want us to understand what they said to each other at meals, my mother and father used to spell their conversation, and that later, when we could follow the spelling, they had to talk French. As neither of them knew more than two or three words of the language, they did not get on very well, and the conversation always ended with my father saying the only whole sentence he really felt confident of, which was: "*Oh, allez au diable!*" And

30

my elder sister used to sit at meals, and no one would notice her until suddenly someone would see the tears rolling down her cheeks.

"What is the matter?" she would be asked.

"I haven't got any potatoes," she would reply in sobs.

My father would look at my mother in astonishment.

"Is the child an idiot?" he would ask her.

I also remember the time when I stood in his bedroom while he was shaving, and he offered me a present, anything I liked to choose. He always gave presents like this, never at Christmas or on birthdays, but when he suddenly felt like it. I said that I had seen a book in a shop called *Bible Steps for Children*, and that it had very fine pictures and I would like that. He frowned in the mirror as he continued to shave.

"I shouldn't think you'd find that very amusing," he said.

But I insisted, and he let me go up the village that morning and buy the book. I never succeeded in reading it, however, because whenever I picked it up, his disappointed, disapproving red face and blue eyes would come between me and it, and I realised he was right and I had made a bad choice.

We used to be dressed all three alike in dark green or red coats and caps, and the curious thing is that I cannot remember that we ever had any friends. There was one other family in the village with children about the same age, but we were never very close to them. And once a year we used to go to a party given by very rich people who lived at Westgate, and there would be a conjuror and dozens of other children, and we simply hated it and used to dread this party for weeks beforehand.

There were the sands, of course, and the sea, and the great bed of green seaweed which, on this part of the coast, used to wash up every summer, and lie rotting and stinking there until some especial tide drew it away. We used to bathe every single day in the summer, no matter what the weather, and very early we learned to play tennis and golf, and I, at any rate, felt the absolute exaltation that physical exercise can give.

But the main thing, the thing that prevents my remembering,

was the strong sense of family security that made the world feel safe. My mother and father used to quarrel terribly, and every morning was announced by the sound of their angry voices in the bathroom. But this meant nothing to us. We thought it was normal. And we used to quarrel terribly ourselves, but this, I think, *was* normal. I am quite sure that I loved both my sisters as well as my father and mother, because any hurt or slight to them caused an astonishing pain at the centre of things, an occasion for a sudden, surprised rush to their defence—the same pain that could stir me to the side of my father until the day of his death.

3

IN *The Shorter Oxford English Dictionary* the word highbrow is given thus:

High browed. 1. Lofty-browed. 2. Intellectually superior, orig. U.S. 1908. So high brow, *a,*; *sb.* a person so characterised 1911.

In the days when it was a fairly new word it was used, at any rate by the lowbrows, in a manner that gave the superiority of the definition a fairly pejorative sense. This may be to some extent true now, but the word has passed into the language, has no longer much freshness and is not highly charged with emotional undertones.

My parents were both lowbrows, and so were all the people who came to their house, and all the people I met as a child. It was an age distinguished above everything by a general philistinism hardly equalled in history, and, although this is difficult to account for, it was so natural that it seems, to me at least, not to have been unattractive. My parents had none of the wistfulness that I and many of my contemporaries feel, the consciousness that there is a richness in life one is untrained to appreciate, but which in other circumstances one might have had the capacity to enjoy. Excluded, it seems, at the age when one might have acquired understanding along with the ability to walk, from the whole world of literature, language, painting, music and philosophy, we know that it is now too late. There are too many things—too many French painters, too many dead languages, too much architecture, sculpture, music, too many eclectic forms of speech and vision, too many traps of every kind —for it to be worth a belated attempt to alter our fate. Sometimes there is the knowledge, too, that if one had been endowed at birth with greater curiosity, the smallest natural taste, a spark of talent, if, even now, one had an enthusiasm which, put to the test, was

33

great enough to bestow the power of concentration, to govern the wandering eye, the unwilling ear and the daydreams which regularly intrude between the mind and the printed page, one might haver idden on it into a world of diverse things that is now denied one. Others have done as much. In America this wistfulness produces the culture vulture, but the English are too self-conscious and have a sense of the ridiculous too highly developed to be able to persuade themselves that one can learn what should be part of the adult understanding, that a little earnest application can make up for years of deprivation in the air one breathed.

Nor did my parents suffer from the anger of those who lack this humility and, lacking it, believe violently in their own inherent talent, seeing always, in any setback, great or small, the same selfish hand that has denied them the tools men in other spheres hold as a right. The angry are forced to scoff, and the scoffer, animated in this way, appears at every level of human intercourse. The farmhand, conscious that by natural ability and a lifetime's experience he has a skill no intellectual process can bestow, watches the boy with the college training placed above him, and is forced to belittle not only the boy but the scientific training that earned him this promotion. His is the hand that breaks the statues, burns the books, turns off the Third Programme.

But my parents were jolly, hearty, robust lowbrows, not lowbrow by accident but by temperament, almost, one might say, superior lowbrows. They thought a highbrow was a highbrow because he had not the levity, wit or natural talent to be anything else; possibly quite nice, but pompous, dull, "stuffy," fair game for the barbed tongues of the more fortunate.

For my mother the heart of the matter lay in an attitude she had acquired I know not where, but which she undoubtedly shared with most other women of her acquaintance. For her the highbrow was a man who might have great taste in poetry, but whose women knew nothing about clothes; who might produce sounds on a musical instrument which transcended human experience,

34

but was a duffer if he asked you to dance; who might talk with the tongue of angels on his own subject, but was stiffly unable to roll the ball of trivialities round a dining-room table; a kind of pathetic, professorial figure of fun to a pair of essentially schoolgirlish eyes. Ultimately it came to this; she believed that, if you were born deficient in physical attraction, you had to make up for it as best you could. And for her, as for all her women friends, physical attractiveness between the sexes, of a superficial, titivated and titillating kind, constituted the major interest in life. Their conversation was the gossip of the senior dormitory in a girls' school, and their taste the taste of the *Tatler* and *Vogue*. They had a stereotyped and simple-minded conception of what constitutes physical attraction in a woman, and a curious but impenetrable belief that very few people outside the circles in which they moved or might have moved were blessed with it. Certainly none of the superior people were. All her life it was impossible to convince my mother that the female members of the aristocracy, as well as of the intellectual groups, did not wear flannel underclothes, and, at times when these become too hot, change to thick if expensive linen. Hers was the opposite of the attitude which finds too much beauty, or intelligence, or charm suspect if not actually vulgar; she thought any aesthetic or ascetic refinement slightly ridiculous, highly undesirable, a bore.

My father's attitude was much less complex, and there was no question with him of subconscious compensation. He simply knew that he could fill a theatre and, at the time of which I write the highbrows could not. He shared, however, with my mother, a tendency to disbelieve that any taste he could not understand was based on anything except pretension.

Ours, then, was a simple society, but not unintelligent. My father never read a book or went to a play he had not written, but my mother did both voraciously. She would have read F. Brett Young, Sheila Kaye-Smith, Gilbert Frankau, Ian Hay, some of Arnold Bennett, possibly a little of H. G. Wells, certainly Somerset Maugham and later on J. B. Priestley, but she would

35

not have heard of E. M. Forster or Virginia Woolf, unless she knew of the Bloomsbury set as a sort of a joke; nor would she have bothered her head with the curiosities of intellectual reading such as P. G. Wodehouse or Edgar Wallace. Late in her life she asked me to explain to her the difference between Evelyn Waugh and Alec Waugh, because, she said, she knew that she liked the books of one but not of the other. I am fairly certain that she had read a good deal of Kipling and Galsworthy but not Dickens, Thackeray or Jane Austen. T. S. Eliot she must have heard of, but I doubt if Auden and Isherwood ever became even names to her. Shakespeare both she and my father regarded as simply a bore, but this was on no evidence whatsoever, and it is possible that, if either of them could have been persuaded into a theatre to hear him, they might have changed their minds. I cannot remember what daily newspapers we took, but none of the weeklies ever entered the house, until we became rather rich, when my mother took the *Sketch*, the *Tatler* and *Vogue*.

During the whole of their lives neither my mother nor my father ever entered a concert hall or an opera house, but when I was quite young we acquired a gramophone. The only two records we had that I can remember now were *If You Were the Only Girl in the World* and *Valse Triste* played by Kreisler. But my husband says it is most unlikely that Kreisler ever played *Valse Triste*, so perhaps there were two different records, one of *Valse Triste* and one of Kreisler playing something else. We used to lie in bed at night and listen to these records being played down below, and up the stairs would float the delicious rich smell of cigar-smoke.

Except for a slight tendency towards sabotage on the part of my father, our religious upbringing was like that of most English children, then and now. We were taught to say our prayers at night, Gentle Jesus and Are Father Whi Chart in Heaven, but this in a fairly perfunctory way. "Hurry up, do, and get into bed." We were taken to church on Christmas Day and occasionally on other days. But there was a complete difference in feeling between my father and my mother on religious matters. My father thought the whole thing bunk, and never at any moment in his whole life did he feel the smallest temptation to depart from this attitude. He was quite unable to understand how any intelligent person could believe in a word of it, and, since he saw no reason why we should be taught it, he was not above winking at us while we were still on our knees repeating our nightly prayers. I have already described how he received my choice of *Bible Steps For Children* as a present. My mother on the other hand had the normal attitude of members of the Church of England. She never went to church herself, and she never read the Bible either to herself or to us; in fact, I doubt whether, before we were old enough to go to school and had to have one, there was a Bible in the house. But she told us the story of Jesus, teaching us to believe in it just as we were taught to believe in Father Christmas, and taught us to say our prayers. She herself believed in God, not very fervently in everyday life and certainly not to her inconvenience, but, like all good Protestants, very fervently at moments when she needed His help.

We were quite young children during the Great War, and, as we lived in the Island of Thanet, on the direct route to London, we were among the first people in the world to experience air-raids. At home in Birchington a neighbour built a deep underground shelter in his garden, possibly highly dangerous, and quite often at night we used to be roused from our sleep and taken down into it, where we were given cups of cocoa, while my father stood at the top of the steps, watching the shrapnel fall. But once, during this period, we were on holiday with my mother at St Margaret's Bay, sleeping at night in the annexe of the hotel, a house which stood high on a hill above the sea with a terraced garden falling sheerly away from it. One night while we were there, we were woken by my mother and made to get up and go into the garden behind the house. In the garden it was entrancing, warm and still under a great moon that made it as light as day. When we looked up, immediately over one corner of the house, it seemed not more than a few hundred feet up, there hung a gigantic cigar-shaped and coloured object. We knew immediately what it was, but I suppose, in spite of our nightly journeys to the air-raid shelter, the extent of its menace had been kept from us, because we were none of us the least frightened. It must have been hit, because it tilted acutely from nose to tail, and we should have liked to go on standing there, enjoying this fantastic scene. But my mother drew us quickly in against the back of the house, holding, I afterwards learned, the view that if it were to be hit it would be bound to fall forwards down the hill, and we would be safer behind it. There, huddled against the back door, she began to pray, chattering to God for ages, imploring Him to take care of us. I remember quite clearly that I was not even then in the very least frightened, but I was horribly shocked and embarrassed. I was only about eight, but I was convinced that this was no way to behave. It was the only serious approach to God I ever heard anyone make during the whole of my childhood, and I did not like it at all. We stayed where we were for what seemed a long time, but presently when someone had the courage to look out, the zeppelin was gone. Soon after this we were sent to a boarding school north of London.

It was a curious incident. My mother was an exceptionally brave woman. Until she was physically incapable of it, she used to hunt, having taken up riding long after she was forty, tearing along at the head of the hunt and riding quite difficult horses; and she was in London during the whole of the second war, giving parties during the height of the blitz, refusing to take shelter or move to the country, and walking with the greatest calmness through the streets of London. That must have been a terrifying moment, alone in a garden with three very young children, and this blown-up instrument of death so near that one felt only a little more and one could touch it. But it was probably her responsibility for us that chiefly unnerved her, and the community courage of the civilians of the second war had not yet developed.

One other irrelevant fact sticks in my memory about this holiday at St Margaret's Bay. When we got home my sister's head was found to be covered with lice. For three whole days my mother washed her head again and again, and combed her hair with a nit-comb, finding, to my shuddering despair, and after much combing and parting of my hair, three nits in my own head. It was thought that the housemaids who had made our beds must have dropped lice on to my sister's pillow.

We were taught to be very good-mannered. My father liked good manners and my mother had this huge sense of what was due to our social position. She placed a quite extraordinary emphasis on our exact place in the social structure. She divided and sub-divided the social classes, and in this I think she was quite correct. No foreigner could ever have understood the degree and extent of the nuances in the society of that time. She placed us amongst the gentry, a class which, according to her, stood between the middle class and the aristocracy. My husband says that pedantically she had some right on her side. Her father was a Colonel in the Royal Artillery and, as such, could not have had his challenge to a duel refused by anyone, whereas, if he had been a business man, it could honourably have been ignored. But since duelling was by now a thing of the past, I cannot imagine how she succeeded in imposing her own view on almost everyone she met. But she did succeed. At all the schools I went to there were two categories of girls, those who received special treatment, since by their presence they attracted the daughters of lesser families, and because they were necessary to the conversations between the headmistresses and the parents of prospective pupils, and all the others. We were always in the first category, and this also meant that, when we were reproved, it was done more in sorrow than anger, with reproachful under-lining of the fact that we, at least, should know better. But if my mother imposed on the simple-minded head-mistresses, I am not sure that she did on her own children. There was among her ancestors a character called Robert Brooke, a small landed proprietor, who served with some distinction in India and was for many years Governor of the Island of St. Helena, and on him she set great store. Such was my aversion to this man that I do not know now whether her father or mother descended from him, and my sisters' dislike of him was quite as great as mine. We used to repeat with burlesqued respect my mother's name: Leslie BROOKE Lonsdale. But what I do not know is whether this attitude took shape in our own rebellious minds, or whether the closing of an eyelid over my father's twinkling blue eye again suggested it to us. Born the son of a Jersey tobacconist, he had an impeccable sense of behaviour, and he would have known by instinct that, whereas it is perfectly all right to comment incessantly on the social position of those below you, always making his exact social flavour the first item in a description of anyone, and conveying in one form of words or another Not Like Us, the heights of one's own position should be taken for granted and never referred to.

In one way, however, she did us a service by her class-consciousness. Although we treated her views with some scepticism, and were considerably embarrassed by her higher flights of fancy, we did not doubt the correctness of her belief that we belonged amongst the higher types of humanity. This gave us a secure sense of superiority, great enough, in fact, to allow us the pleasure of ridiculing her. We had not that absurd and irrational feeling of family importance which many people seem to have, that our family was *the* family, and not to belong to it in itself a natural handicap, but we had a pleasant pride in ourselves. And for children to feel superior for the wrong reasons is happier than for them not to feel superior at all.

But if there was something lacking in the intellectual and spiritual atmosphere of my home, this was more than made up for in stimulus on the periphery of the third great pre-occupation of mankind. When we were children we used to sit about the room when my mother's friends were in the house, listening to their conversation. Quite young we knew all there was to know of their views on men, on other women, on clothes and make-up, and we learned quickly to detect, if not completely to interpret, the phrases they used when they did not wish us to understand them. It was not for long necessary, either, for us to use our wits to discover what we wanted to know, because at an exceedingly early age, when I was not more than eleven, my mother began to make us her confidantes in all her affairs, and to talk to us much as she talked to these other women.

Quite early in their married life my father was unfaithful to her, although it was some years before she found this out. I have the, possibly romantic, idea that, when she did find it out, it changed her character. In any case, she was exceedingly lonely at times and always resentful. There was never any question of her leaving my father or even of her making much effort to limit his actions. At this time he did not wish her to leave him, and he always used his abominable charm without honesty or pity to achieve his own ends. He was the only person I have known who was exactly like a character in a novel, Lewis in *The Constant Nymph*, or one of those unbelievable artists whose wives put up with endless upheavals and provocation because the understanding between them is of an ultimate kind. But my mother was not in the least like a character in a novel, and, although she never ceased to love him, her resentment became consuming.

When it comes to affairs of the heart, there are few women who find it possible to restrain themselves from making confidences to other women. When they are happy they can sometimes maintain a smug reticence, but let the least thing go wrong, let the telephone once not ring when it is expected to, or a letter fail to arrive, and the compulsion becomes too great; they rush piteously off to the woman who at the time is nearest to them. My mother lived in a small village beside the sea and was often without feminine companionship for weeks on end. And so, since she had to talk to someone, she talked to her children. We always knew exactly what my father was up to, with whom, and what my mother thought about it. Because she loved and admired him, she did not turn us against him, but she did make us believe that the enormity and unexpectedness of his crimes could be forgiven him only because his talents made him abnormal. We did not think of him as a monster, but we regarded her as quite exceptionally unlucky and ill-treated. And we did not question until years later the right this gave her to exploit him by every means in her power.

41

In the years immediately following the war we moved into our fifth and last house in Birchington. It was built on the edge of the cliff and steps from our garden led straight down on to the beach. It had a large drawing-room.

Birchington had now become an exceedingly popular holiday place. This was the beginning of the dancing years, when men and women of all ages took up dancing with a kind of compulsive idiocy which can be explained only by the depth of their revulsion from the horror of the war years. In Birchington all summer long there were dances every night of the week in the hotels, and on Sundays these were continued in the drawing-room of our house. My elder sister and I, aged thirteen and twelve, always attended these dances, dressed in exceedingly pretty clothes. It was a loose and frivolous society, composed largely of married people bent on having their fling, with plenty of young men from a neighbouring aerodrome, some girls of marriageable age, my sister and myself. Sometimes there were other children too, both girls and boys. We joined in everything with precocious competence. We knew, or thought we knew, the form-book thoroughly—exactly who was having an affair with whom, who was jealous, who must not be interrupted when dancing together. We also had, as dancing partners, an enormous success ourselves. My mother said that this was because, not being of marriageable age, we were perfectly safe and restful for the young men. But, looking back on it, and remembering how all the old men used also to fight to dance with us, I am not sure that this judgment was not a trifle naive. In any case, it was when, on the same evening, my mother overheard one young lady say to another: "It's never amusing until these damned Lonsdale children go to bed," and my sister reply to a learned counsel who had asked her to dance: "Thank you so much. Missing fifteen," that she decided for the second time to send us to boarding school.

But for several months before that evening we enjoyed ourselves enormously and learned a great deal about life. We were never in any danger of learning from personal experience, partly because we were perfectly ordinary middle-class children and very prudish, but also because my father, who was the person responsible for our presence there, nevertheless watched us with an insanely suspicious care. If either of us was out of the room for ten minutes he would start prowling round the garden looking for her, usually to find her on his return still dancing, having merely been upstairs. If by chance he found either of us actually in the garden taking the air, he would return in fury and hiss the blackest suggestions into my mother's ear. All of this she repeated to us the next morning, so that the possibilities of horror and wickedness in the society of men were early implanted in our minds, although evidence of the pleasures of it was continually before our eyes. For this society, which formed itself fortuitously and only in the summer months, had no cohesion, no stimulus and no reason except the pursuit of pleasure through ephemeral engagements with members of the opposite sex. What distinguished it from any other society I have known were the scale and deliberateness of the intention, and also the fact that none of these men or women was looking for love or even for passion, but only for excitement and an indulgence of vanity.

On the part of the women it was a free-for-all, in which each stood alone and fought for place with every weapon she had. No considerations of friendship or pity ever intervened in what was, it seems to me now, an unspeakably vulgar competitive game. This was in the aftermath of the war and during a financial boom, so that these people who were driven, one can only presume, to this burst of triviality by the horrors they had lately lived through, also had the money to pay for it. But the complete lack of humanity or dignity on the part of these married couples seems to me to have stemmed from earlier traditions. Victorian morality was not yet entirely discarded and the cuckolds were usually preserved from knowledge of their fate. I could not have so certain a picture of what took place behind the scenes had not all the women talked to each other and my mother talked to us. And if the behaviour of these women was

43

less elegant, it does not seem in standards or values to have been very different from those of the great Edwardian society.

My mother acquired what she referred to as "experience." "Ah!" she would say to us when we were seventeen and eighteen, looking at our rosy cheeks, "if only one had your skins and my experience." This experience was simply a set of rules for putting men through the hoops, titillating them to the point and torturing them into remaining there. My mother's generation had no shame in applying these rules, and very little shame in anything else. In my youth it was constantly said and apparently believed that no woman could have a genuine friendship for another woman, and mine was the first generation that regarded (with the help of birth control) the cuckoo in the nest as an offence against manners and taste. And if it was the spread of medical science as much as anything else that altered our morals, the fact is that they did alter, and it is by the strength of our revulsion against this older society that both the cynicism and the romanticism of our own can be explained. Generosity we believed was more beautiful than chastity, truth nobler than respectability, and honour in personal relationships more important than either. These rather sentimental themes can be found in many of the plays and books of our youth.

I have recently read two of the plays which, soon after this, were to have enormous success on the London stage, and which depicted a society inconceivable now—*Our Betters* by Somerset Maugham and *The Vortex* by Noel Coward. In *Our Betters* the author brings on to the stage a cast of people who, at first sight, might have stepped out of a novel by Henry James—Lady Grayston, the Duchesse de Surennes, the Principessa della Cercola, Elizabeth Saunders, Arthur Fenwick, Thornton Clay, Fleming Harvey, Anthony Paxton, Lord Bleane, Pole and Ernest. Most of the characters are of American birth, and Elizabeth Saunders and Fleming Harvey are innocent, but here the resemblance ends. For this is a predatory society without manners, heart or taste, pursuing pleasure with the single-minded vulgarity that I remember at Birchington, and finding it only through the

44

body and through vanity. Somerset Maugham was concerned with the problems of rich American women married to the European aristocracy, but the play was acted nightly to English audiences which found it credible and interesting. The author, a dramatist of great bitterness and power, introduces two characters I do not remember to have met in my childhood, but who could later be seen in the night-clubs of London and more especially in the pleasure resorts of the Riviera—the first a gigolo, a young man kept by an ageing, hungry woman, and paid quite directly in money for the attentions he bestowed, the second a professional dancing-master, a power amongst the women. There is a scene in which Lady Grayston and the gigolo, hotting up suddenly on the stage, prepare to betray his benefactor, the Duchesse de Surennes, which still reads with a sultry strength. And yet I do not believe this play can live. There is no tragedy and no genuine comedy, because this hard-faced, hard-hearted society has no depth, no emotions, no desires and no thought which are of the slightest interest out of the context of the strange years in which the play was set.

The Vortex introduces members of a similar society, and here again we meet the gigolo. This play is also still interesting because of the flippant but genuine wit of the author (the talent of the 1920s for the dialogue of social comedy seems to me to have been far greater than anything we hear now), but the problem of the play, the emotions of the beautiful, ageing mother and her neurotic, degenerate and mildly drug-taking son, are of an unreality and of a boredom that makes one wonder how it was ever possible to sit through it. In *The Vortex,* too, they dance incessantly, most of the dialogue and much of the action taking place against the continuous shuffle of couples locked in each other's embrace, the stage directions giving much consideration to how the lines are to be heard against the background of the eternal gramophone.

My father always wanted to have us with him. This is the explanation of our being allowed at so young an age to the dances at Birchington. As we grew older we entered more and more into his life. We were taught to play golf by professionals, and by the time we were twelve we played tennis quite well enough to join in a four with him and his friends. All summer long we used to play golf at St Augustine's or at Prince's at Sandwich, and tennis on the public courts in front of the Bungalow Hotel at Birchington, but always with grown-up people. In the winter I used to walk with him every day. This was an entirely one-way traffic, because at no time in his life was he prepared to be even civil to the young people who might have been suitable for us. When we came home from school for the week-end my mother always used to greet us with the same joke: "Now what shall we do that will be amusing for Daddy's half-term?" We knew actors, writers, lawyers, doctors, but almost no one of our own age. And because he was aware of the terms on which he enjoyed our society, my father grew more and more anxious about our future.

These were the days when there were too few men in the world and too few jobs. The natural desire of parents to see their daughters married was considerably heightened not merely by these circumstances, but also because, with the break-up of society after the war, marriage, while by no means inevitable, seemed to offer greater opportunities than ever before. Watching their three little daughters grow, all very near in age, none especially shining, and aware of their limitations as parents, my mother and father became obsessed by this subject long before we were of marriageable age. I can remember no time when I was not aware of being anxiously watched, hopefully considered, and no time when I was unconscious that life was gathering force for the moment of surmounting this exquisite hazard. Conscious, too, that in the life he had chosen for us to lead there might be dangers, my father, who in any case was pathologically suspicious, guarded our virtue with the frenzied and suggestive fervour of a maniac. He was determined that when the great competitive moment came we should still retain the only armour he deemed necessary. Marriage, it was drummed into us by every means in his power, and long before we properly under-stood the concept, was only for virgins. Until the right man came

46

along we must fight off every attention, trust no one, and learn to look after ourselves. He never spoke directly to us on this subject, but he nagged incessantly at my mother, forcing her to impart his views to us, and, commenting on life for our instruction, he did all he could to help her. Here is a story he told in front of me when I was about sixteen.

A woman, walking upstairs to a flat, stumbled and nearly fell.

"My darling," said her companion, putting out his arm to help her, "do be more careful. You might hurt yourself."

Later, walking down the stairs, she stumbled again.

"For Christ's sake," the man said then, "don't you ever walk up or down stairs without falling?"

This was meant to be immensely putting off, and no doubt it would have been if I had understood it. Actually it was some years before I remembered this story and burst out laughing at his absurdity.

In spite of all this I was constantly in love as a child. The first time was at the age of about eight, when I fell in love with an actor called Edmund Gwenn, watching him play Shock-headed Peter. For weeks afterwards I mooned about for him, but this caused so much affectionate ridicule that I soon learned to keep my love-life to myself. The second time was also with an actor, one of a party of people who used to come and bathe on the shore beneath our house. For weeks I used to sit near him on the sands, hoping that one day he would speak to me. He never did. Mostly I was in love with very tall men between the ages of twenty and thirty, but on two occasions I loved people I had never seen. The first time I had an exceptional success. There was a house between us and Westgate of which I remember nothing except that outside the brick walls there was mown grass surrounded by white posts and chains. Inside this house there lived a woman whose son was away somewhere in the army. For no reason at all I simply fell in love with him. But presently, when he returned on leave he told his mother, after seeing me once, that he would never marry until I grew old enough. The second time was less successful. For months my heart was lost to an actress who was playing in one of my father's plays, but whom I had never seen. One day he took me to a rehearsal, and I sat in the front row of the stalls gazing passionately at her. But after the rehearsal was over and my father suggested to her some alteration in her performance, she turned on him in a rage and said: "I suppose your daughter, who never smiled once, told you this." And it was said that, rebuking one of the chorus girls for a miserable and unrequited feeling for my father, she said; "You need not waste any time on Freddy Lonsdale. He never has and never will love anyone but that odious little daughter." I also fell in love with the older girls at school, but the *Schwärmerei* being very badly viewed in my family, thought silly as well as unnatural, all these secrets I kept locked in my own heart. None of this seems to have been in any way out of the ordinary. Many women have told me that their capacity for love was far greater in their childhood than at any other time.

4

THE education of female children in England has never been considered a matter of much importance, and was always the perquisite of the maiden lady, the poor relation. When I was a child the exercise of this natural right grew to the size of a swindle.

There was a superfluity of women. There was also mass unemployment and, in the aftermath of the war, the break-up of the structure of the old society. There were no jobs for the unqualified and the unintelligent, and practically no openings for women. The impoverished spinsters of England, many of whom might, before the war, have found a place in the shadows of some great household, were thrown out into the world to fend for themselves. They had, it seemed, only one unquestioned right, to teach the female children of the upper and upper-middle classes to grow up as inept and as mentally indigent as they were themselves. This right they exploited on a great scale. All over England maiden ladies with a little capital started up schools for girls, in which they employed as staff maiden ladies without capital.

In the days when these poor women had been asked to teach only two or three children at a time, in houses where there might be a civilised environment, parents with intellectual tastes to guide them, music, pictures, books, they had not necessarily failed entirely in their task of stimulating the developing mind. In some pleasant, shabby schoolroom, looking out over a garden, a book read out loud round the fire or the visit of some distinguished guest might do much to provoke curiosity, or to start some interesting discussion. But when, chosen usually for their own great need and their willingness to accept the meanest salaries, they grouped together to take charge of sixty or seventy children, the impertinence of their undertaking went unrecognised only because of the unexacting nature of the demands made by the parents. It was the children alone who were swindled.

Nowadays there is much talk of how the educational system of England—in particular the great public schools—has imposed, and is responsible for maintaining, the undemocratic class-structure. In my day and for my sex nothing but the class-structure could have made possible the educational system.

The schools I attended had to be Schools for Young Ladies, the parents had to be subjected to searching enquiries during the first interview, one peer's daughter had to be acquired as a pupil and her father's name retained on the list of patrons—these few simple rules observed and a comfortable income was assured. My parents, along with the parents of most of my contemporaries, had only one requirement in return for fees that would have kept their sons at Eton: that we should be turned into marriageable young ladies. If it is wondered why this delicate task was hopefully entrusted to those who had so singularly failed in it themselves (and indeed the more precocious of their pupils were astonished at their lack of even the smallest knowledge of the necessary arts), the answer is that, consciously or unconsciously, it was believed that the only possible improvement that could be made upon nature was to preserve us from all contact with children of the lower social orders.

I went altogether to five of these schools, and three of them made exceptional claims when it came to the teaching of French. This meant that instead of this subject being taught by an impoverished Englishwoman, it was taught by an impoverished and sour, because expatriate, Frenchwoman. For half my life I hated the whole French nation in return for the samples of their race they sent over to teach me their language. Those of my contemporaries whose parents were richer than mine were usually sent to a finishing school in Paris when they were sixteen or seventeen. In this way, but in this way only, my education fell below that of many of my generation and class.

At the inkstained desks of those schools we sat pinioned by

boredom, while there took place around us what can only be described as the tittle-tattle, the merest gossip of education. Looking back, it seems to me that the whole of my schooling was simply a series of lists. Who wrote: *Lorna Doone, The Bible in Spain, The Mill on the Floss*? What are the principal towns, rivers, exports, of the Argentine? I have sometimes wondered whether there was ever any purpose in these lists other than the obvious one of passing the time. Certainly no one ever suggested that one might want to visit the rivers of the Argentine, or read *The Mill on the Floss*. If there was a purpose, it was doubtless pretentious. It cannot have been imagined that when, at a party for debutantes, the young men fell into a discussion of *The Bible in Spain*, the murmuring of the words George Borrow would suggest that here, in an odd, rather blue-stocking form, was a marriageable girl. But it might have been thought that a spirited and quick-witted young lady could use these wisps of knowledge to create, when it might be appreciated, an appearance of culture where none in fact existed.

I was taught somewhere, I suppose, the three Rs, but even that is true only on the most simple definition. When, at the beginning of the war, Coney Jarvis, Mary Dunn and I put ourselves back to school at a Farm Institute, I had to persuade Jimbo Lubbock to explain to me the working of the decimal system before I could follow the lectures, and I had to impart the information he gave me to both Mary and Coney, whose schooldays took place later than mine. We were all three astonished to find there was no difficulty, but, on the other hand, we had to give up one subject—Survey—altogether because we could not acquire a knowledge of algebra.

Certainly I was never taught the principles of English grammar. Such terms as the subjunctive or the past participle have no meaning for me, and, quite recently, when I was trying to explain something to my eldest daughter, she explained to me that I did not understand the difference between an adverb and a preposition.

As a child I never, so far as I know, saw a painting by an old

51

master, nor even a reproduction except those that were used on hoardings for advertising. We were taught drawing at school, and I remember sitting for hours squinting along the side of a pencil, which I held vertically in front of my face, at a jug on a table. But I have forgotten what was the point of the squinting, although I think there was one.

Nor, except on one occasion, did I hear any music. The last of the schools I went to was owned by an elderly Belgian lesbian who also had a school just outside Brussels. It was one day decided to take six of the eldest girls from the English school for a few weeks to the Belgian one, and I was amongst them. The great moment for the time we spent there, the thing we all most looked forward to, was a visit to the opera-house to hear *The Marriage of Figaro*. Two of the six girls were South Africans, and naturally very musical. They had very pretty voices and were in great demand because they used to sing popular songs in harmony together. But they, like the rest of us, had never before been to the opera or to a concert-hall.

We were all very excited and I remember that, the night before we were to go, Leonora Wodehouse did up her hair in an arrangement of curlers that looked extremely uncomfortable. In the night she dreamed that she was already at the opera, and a disgrace to the whole party, as she had somehow arrived there without having taken out the curlers. So stealthily she removed the whole lot, and woke up next morning with her hair in its natural condition. We also played truant during the day, when we were supposed to be looking at the architectural beauties of Brussels, so as to buy shoes that would grace our best dresses.

When the great moment came we sat, a line of six girls, in the stalls, breathlessly excited. Half-way through the first act I looked down the row at the faces of the others. Everyone was rigid with boredom. No one moved. It was a situation we were accustomed to and could easily bear, but all the disconsolate mouths and the glances that returned my own spoke of the disappointment. None of us was able to distinguish anything from the conglomerate sounds.

We were, however, taught some music. We learned the piano. At the end of seven years' instruction Leonora Wodehouse could play The Merry Peasant, and after learning for about the same time, on an occasion when half the senior school was in bed with flu, I was commanded to play the hymns in chapel one evening. I was very pleased with this assignment, and all day I practised the three hymns I had to play at a piano in one of the bedrooms, deaf to the voices of the other girls and to all attempts to persuade me away. When I arrived in the chapel I could play all the hymns with complete accuracy, but not quite fast enough. Another difficulty was that, such was the effort of concentration required, I could not, in addition to providing the accompaniment, count the number of times I played each verse. All went well during the first two hymns, because the congregation were friends, and, after some surprise at the start, they loyally accepted the tempo. When I came to the end of the last verse, the girl nearest me dropped her prayer-book with a bang beside me, and I played the Amen. But the third hymn, being the least practised, was the most difficult, and so lost was I in my efforts that, when the prayer-book dropped, I failed to notice it, and, after the last verse had been sung several times, my performance had to be terminated by force. No one had ever suggested to the Wodehouses or to my parents that the money spent on our piano-lessons might reasonably be saved.

The time was to come, too, when I would feel that I could have forgiven these pathetic women their failure to teach me the academic arts if they had taught the more feminine ones. To know how to sew, or to cook, to wash, to iron and to mend, even to pack one's own clothes without crumpling them, to have the smallest idea what process cleans out a bath—for any of these necessary pieces of knowledge I might willingly have traded the whole world of intellectual pleasures. But in those days such tasks were regarded as essentially menial, the lower classes were there to perform them (no one apparently heeded the signs that they were ceasing to be), and later, when my mother employed a maid to walk behind me, picking up my clothes and tidying my cupboards, she indulged me and her pride no more than was common at the time.

While we were at day-school we went to church on Sundays less and less often, and finally never at all. But when we were at boarding school we had to go regularly. We must have gone when we were at the school at Teddington during the war, but I cannot remember anything about it, not even the appearance or position of the church. The church at Bromley, when we were much older, is seared on my memory. I know now that the ceremony we attended there was of a Low Church kind. The vicar was a very tall, shabby, old man, and almost gaga. He must always have had a distressing, jowly appearance, and in his old age he had developed two sets of deep channels on his face, one pair from his cheeks to his mouth and the other from his mouth to his chin. He sniffed constantly and a permanent small stream of saliva flowed down the two lower channels to his chin. Every Sunday morning he indulged himself for half an hour in the pulpit. This was the most agonising experience of the whole of my schooldays. It was not that he was so much more boring than, for instance, the Frenchwomen, but in the classroom one could always enliven matters with a running fire of silly questions, while in church one had to keep quiet. I developed a burning hatred for this old man, which I think accounts for the fact that I can never enter a church during a service without my hackles beginning to rise.

He came every year to our school to prepare girls for confirmation. The year that the age-group included myself and my friends, we laid on for him the same delicate operation we used to relieve the boredom in school. This consisted of asking questions with a double meaning, but to conduct it successfully required a neat technique. The second meaning had to be very obvious, because otherwise there was a high probability that the unsophisticated maiden ladies would miss it. But it had to be so firmly covered with a first meaning that they dare not refer or object to the second, for fear of suggesting something to young minds that were genuinely innocent. Any girl whose question provoked a

54

suspicious response immediately looked so completely blank that the attack was withdrawn in a flurry of embarrassment; but she was not so highly marked as if she had caused simply a second of hesitant thought.

The vicar turned out to be no fun at all; he merely sniffed and slobbered and grunted and returned to what he was ineffectually trying to say. When in the third of his classes, a question we were all intensely proud of, and which I still think unanswerable to a roomful of schoolgirls—if we are all descended from Adam and Eve, whom did Cain marry?—fell completely flat, I felt I could stand no more. The following morning I went to see the headmistress and explained to her that I did not wish to be confirmed as I had doubts on the matter. I was amazed by her reply. I had expected to have to withdraw my objections in some disgrace, but, on the contrary, I was admired and praised for my moral courage. Emboldened by this success, I asked whether, during the time that I should now have free, someone could be found to teach me shorthand. This also provoked a scene of admiration, and, much to the disgust of every other girl, I not only had a quite amusing lesson while they sat with the dribbling old man, but I was openly cherished for my daring conduct.

The following year I made the same explanation and the same request. But what is original and courageous once, becomes simply tiresome when it is made a habit. I was firmly and shortly dealt with, and afterwards both prepared and confirmed against my will. On the morning after the confirmation, I went to communion for the first and last time in my life. Nevertheless, I had not yet lost my belief in God, and did not completely until about twenty years later. But this church and the disgusting old vicar had a lasting effect, and I think it possible that, but for him, I might still be among the faithful, because there are certain things in the Christian religion I find it difficult not to believe. I decided to reject the whole thing only when I found I could no longer stomach the normal English approach to religion, and yet was insufficiently enthusiastic for a more scrupulous attitude. I think that I shall never return to the Church, but on the other hand I am not amongst those who marvel at the weak minds of the believers.

The first school we went to was a small kindergarten in Birchington. I remember only two things about it, and the first took place out of school. Beside the railway bridge there are, or were, some high wooden railings with a high half-gate which leads to the steps that go down to the station. One day I was performing a feat on these railings which I was very proud of, and which I referred to as vaulting. It was not vaulting in the sense of jumping with the aid of one hand and arm right over the top, but consisted of climbing the first two rails, leaning over, placing one hand on the further side of the middle rail, and then swinging one's fat bottom and legs onto the other side. I was immensely pleased with my ability to perform this feat, because, although I was always average at games, at gymnastics I was simply a mass of strong, inelastic muscles. Whatever the physique of a ballet dancer, mine is the opposite. While I was enjoying myself showing off in this way, the headmistress of the kindergarten passed, and, evidently genuinely shocked, rebuked me severely for behaving improperly while a member of her school. I was not only angry, I was aghast at what I conceived to be an insufferable piece of impertinence. I was not at the time under her charge but under that of my parents, and I was quite well enough aware of her social position in relation to ours to feel that she was exceeding her powers in attempting to give me instruction on the propriety or impropriety of any behaviour my parents had allowed. I was pleased and soothed to notice the blank faces and lifted eyebrows of my mother and father when I reported this incident.

The second thing I remember is standing in a half-circle with about twenty other very young children, for the first time bent on that kind of diversion which, in one form or another, was to enliven the whole of my school life. We began to sing a nursery rhyme:

> *Ding Dong Dell,*
> *Pussy's in the well.*

> *Who put her in?*
> *Little Tommy Thin.*
> *Who pulled her out?*
> *Little Tommy Stout.*

But when we got to the last line, we sang in a triumphant chorus, not Little Tommy Stout, but Little Brussel Sprout.

We must have had a nice, open diction, for the piano stopped immediately, and the woman teaching us rose with awe-inspiring severity to her feet.

"Who sang the wrong words?" she asked.

I am very truthful. I cannot help it. So I immediately said that I had. One other child did the same. The two of us, by now very scared, were dragged by the arm from the circle of children into an unused and cold room, where, although nothing else happened to us, we were left for the rest of the morning, growing more and more frightened, while I also worked up a tremendous anger against my elder sister, who had sung Little Brussel Sprout, as had every other child, but had not owned up. On the way home to luncheon, after we had finally been released, I beat her and said that I thought her behaviour was beastly, and we arrived home in tears, I from righteous indignation, and she from the terrible bullying she had received. My mother listened to my version of the story, while my sister continued to sob. After luncheon my mother went to the school, taking my sister with her, and there my sister owned up. She was a pretty and a highly nervous child, and her piteous looks evoked much sympathy—a persistent unfairness which throughout our childhood caused me to beat her continually. Now, as on many other occasions, she evaded all punishment; all was forgiven and forgotten. But not by my mother. The following term we went to school at a convent in Westgate.

It is not quite fair to count this convent among the schools responsible for my education, because we were there so short a time that I remember only one thing about it. That is the horrible break at eleven o'clock in the morning, a recurrently painful memory of the first term at each of my schools, when, standing in a courtyard either alone or with one of my sisters, we had to put up a performance of enjoying ourselves madly, while everyone else in the school played and shouted around us and ignored our presence absolutely. But this is one of the few lessons I do not hold against my schooldays; it is so often useful in life to have practised it early. The second reason why it is not fair to count this convent school is that I think, if the humble nuns had been given a chance, they would have taught us more than their secular sisters ever did.

But soon after this the shadow of the great zeppelin loomed over us and we were sent to a school in Teddington. This was a very bad school even for those days, and certainly I learned nothing there except, as a girl guide, how to tell the difference between a reef knot and a granny; this is a question of twisting the cord the second time one way or another, and nowadays I can never remember which way. While we were there my mother used to come regularly at the week-end to see us, and we used always to go to Hampton Court, where we loved the state rooms and the court with the signs of the zodiac, and the maze and the great vine. Afterwards we used to go to a tea-shop by the river, where we ate a sponge cake surmounted by tinned apricots. I think my mother must have brought this with her. One day my father came by himself to see us. His projected visit threw us into a terrible flurry, and after much thought we decided the only thing to do was to wait hidden by the front door so that we could rush out and intercept him before he could meet the headmistress, an old Frenchwoman named Madame Mottu. When a car arrived and we saw him get out, we flung ourselves down the steps and I, as the spokesman, seized him by the arm before he had finished paying the taxi.

"Daddy," I implored him, "please, please don't be funny with Madame Mottu."

Since at the time he was earning a very big income being funny in several of the theatres of London, he chose to treat our entreaty as a very good joke, and could be heard repeating it for years afterwards. I was at this school when the armistice was declared, for some reason on a playing field when at eleven o'clock sirens went off and people rushed by shouting out the news. I felt very constrained because I knew that I ought to feel some emotion, just as I ought to have done when my grandfather died, but, although on that occasion I had screwed out some tears by sitting beside a hot fire and concentrating on the matter, this time I could achieve nothing. I was uncertain exactly what kind of emotion I ought to try for.

Now that the danger was over we left this school and for several years went as day-girls to a school in Westgate. This was very nasty and very snobbish and, from the only point of view that mattered, far the most successful of all my schools. There were at least two earls' daughters and two future marchionesses among the pupils, and the teaching reached the depths of the whole of my experience. We used, all three of us by now, to bicycle each morning along the coast-road from Birchington to Westgate, and so much did we hate going to school that we spent half the day playing truant, having punctures or falling off and cutting our knees, or, if all else failed, simply going into Westgate and hanging about until we felt we had missed at least two of the lessons. Everyone found this very difficult to deal with, because my father, who had played truant from school during the whole of his childhood, regarded it as, at last, a sign that we had inherited something of his audacious nature; and, as he had a complete contempt for learning, he thought that the more we could evade it the better. It was this truancy as much as the dancing that finally convinced my mother we would be better at boarding school.

At this next school, the one at which I was confirmed, there was one woman on the staff, the only one I ever met, who had a talent for teaching. She also had a love, blind and completely humourless but still a love, for English literature. I might have learned a great deal from her, because she warmed to me for trying hard with my essays. She always wrote on the bottom of my page Very Good Indeed or Excellent, and, when I suddenly answered in class questions no one else had bothered to listen to, she looked across the room at me with love. But there was a great barrier between us. On the bloodshot whites of her eyes there were a number of small orange spots joined together by a delicate orange tracery, as though some small golden snail had passed that way, and I was unable to look at her, or respond to the encouragement and friendship she longed to give me.

So the only thing I learned which much influenced my life was how to inhale cigarette-smoke and become a chain-smoker. This was taught me in the garden on Sundays by a Hungarian girl, who had smoked at home since the age of twelve and was seriously inconvenienced by the school rules.

I was always happy at school. I had then an extrovert and enthusiastic nature, and I was never homesick, unlike my two sisters, one of whom wept herself away from school before she was sixteen, while the other merely took a train to London one evening in the middle of term, and was allowed by my father to stay there. I enjoyed the society of my contemporaries, and, although I was always in trouble for bumptiousness during my first term at every school, the qualities which made for this difficulty always turned out, like showing off, to be just the thing in the second term. I was also naturally bossy, and, as I grew older, I enjoyed being one of the head girls and the captain of games.

But when the great moment came and I looked for the last time on these classrooms, I did so without love or respect, and without the smallest idea that there might be something here to regret. I stepped forward hopefully and trustfully, as untended as a wild flower that shoots out of a hedge, to meet the adventure of life.

It cannot have been many years after this that Virginia Woolf was to write *A Room of One's Own*, the most brilliant and moving appeal for the education and freedom of women. In this book she said:

"Women have served all these centuries as looking-glasses possessing the magic and delicious power of reflecting the figure of man at twice its natural size. Without that power probably the earth would still be swamp and jungle. The glories of all our wars would be unknown. . . . How is he to go on giving judgement, civilising natives, making laws, writing books, dressing up and speechifying at banquets, unless he can see himself at breakfast and at dinner at least twice the size he really is? . . . The looking-glass vision is of supreme importance because it charges the vitality; it stimulates the nervous system."

Since these words were written much has changed, but the change would have been far greater were it not that for nine out of every ten women the most desirable function in life, the one pleasure they could never forgo, is to serve as a looking-glass. And this, I think, will always be so. But if throughout the centuries we are to continue to play our chosen part, shall we shine with the bright empty light of a Woolworth mirror? How much better if, polished and subtle, in frames made perhaps in Venice, or carved in the classical manner in England, or painted and gilded in France, or capricious and rococo, we could reflect all these scientists with the rich and subdued glow of an older civilisation.

5

A LITTLE while ago at the house of a friend someone spilt some champagne, and I, continuing to talk, automatically dipped my fingers in it and dabbed them behind my ears.

"Ah!" said my host. "Brought up in a night-club."

And he was right.

I left school when I was a little less than seventeen, and for a few months my future was in doubt. There was a suggestion that I should be sent, as so many of my contemporaries were, to be finished in Paris, but there were several reasons against it. The most important, I think, must have been that this was one of the times when my father had very little money. Soon after this he was to make a fortune in the theatre, and there had already been times when he was very well-off; but he was a spendthrift of heroic proportions, and so lazy and uncalculating that he was often unable to do any work until driven to it by the actual or imminent presence of the bailiffs in the house. Several years before this he had certainly earned enormous sums from a musical comedy called *The Maid of the Mountains*, but the big cheques paid weekly to his bank prevented his doing any work for seven years. In any case, I remember that in my last term at school I had written to my mother telling her that I had an invitation to go to London for the week-end with a schoolfriend, but that I should have to have money for my fare, and a little in case I needed it in London. She replied by sending me a half-crown wrapped up in cotton wool in an envelope with a message that she was sorry it was all she could afford.

The second thing which prevented my being sent to Paris was that my father liked my presence at home, and, having a contempt for all learning, could see no reason why he should be deprived of me in the interests of my being able to talk French. But the third and conclusive influence was my own determination to remain at home and begin the adult life to which I had so expectantly looked forward.

Nevertheless, the question of my future was not yet definitely settled when Sir Patrick Hastings became Attorney-General in the first Labour Government ever to hold power in England, and told my father that, since he needed an extra secretary to deal with the work produced by his social and parliamentary engagements, he would give me a job. This was the result of my having learned a little shorthand at school instead of taking the confirmation classes, an action which had been much admired at home as well as briefly at school.

The two things I remember best about my job as secretary to the Attorney-General are the solicitude of two Irish policemen at the House of Commons that I should keep it, and the determination of Sir Patrick Hastings's clerk that I should lose it. Sir Patrick was a curious character. One of the leading counsel of his day, he might be said to have been the greatest exponent of one of the two methods normally used by barristers in court, both of which would almost certainly alienate the sympathies of a jury of today. In those days counsel were either theatrical or bullying, and when employing the latter method, there seems to have been no limit to the amount juries would stand. Quite recently I threw away unfinished a life of Lord Carson because his biographer quoted, apparently with approval and relish, the story of an occasion on which the great man, during the course of an action, turned on a man employed as a chauffeur, who had committed no crime other than that of being the witness of an event of importance, and no offence except that of trying to protect himself from an irrelevant and personal question about his own private life, and used the authority of his position, as well as his magnificent presence and caustic wit, to cow this man into subservience. But the leading, most intractable bully in court was not Lord Carson, but Sir Patrick Hastings. He could also be terrifying in ordinary society, and he had, in addition to a bullying manner, a strange and often incomprehensible sense of humour.

I was once present when he rose to his feet at a public dinner given to raise funds for some charity, the appeal for which he was there to support, and delivered a speech in which he guyed at some length, not merely the purposes of the charity, but also those guests at the dinner from whom the largest contributions were expected.

But this relentless, insensitive, public figure was, in the privacy of his family and to the few people he loved, one of the kindest and gentlest of men. I had known him all my life, and to me he was, in the fashion of those days, "Uncle Pat," a person whom it was safe to love and trust absolutely, affectionate, humorous and kind.

My job with him was the only one of my life I was unable to take seriously. I was supposed to go to the House of Commons every day at four o'clock, and there take down in shorthand letters to his constituents or answers to invitations, and letters about other small matters of little importance. At six o'clock I would go home, and there I was supposed to type these letters during the next day, taking them back on the following afternoon for him to sign. All this would have been very well if there had been anything to do; but there was almost nothing. Sometimes there would be a few letters, but often I would just sit about in his room while he talked to people who came to see him, and sometimes I was sent to sit outside the room while he discussed matters of importance and secrecy with some other great man. Often too he came very late from the Law Courts, and I had nothing to do but read my book while waiting for him. So after a time I gave up my first feeling of serious importance, and bothered very little about any of the rules, even that of punctuality. I used to arrive at the door of St Stephen's any time between four and half-past four that suited me, and there on most days I would stop and talk to a friendly Irish policeman, who was bored by his waiting job himself. Then I would saunter on, and, stopping again at the door of the main hall, gossip again with another policeman, who also by chance was Irish. But occasionally when I arrived at St Stephen's, the policeman would be waiting for me with a stern face of trouble. Stepping forward to meet me, he would cry:

"Hurry, hurry! He's here. He went in ten minutes ago, and you're late."

When he said this and I noted his anxious, friendly concern, to oblige him I would run like a mad thing on my very high heels all the way up the long corridor to where the second policeman waited with the latest bulletin.

"It's all right," he would sometimes say. "He's gone in with the Solicitor-General, and he doesn't even know you're not here."

But when he called out, as the other one had, "Hurry! Hurry! You're late, you're late," I would run on diagonally across the great hall, through the door half-right, and, thumping through a second door, arrive scarlet and panting in the Attorney-General's office.

The first time I did this, Uncle Pat looked up from the papers he was reading.

"What on earth is the matter?" he asked.

And so I explained to him that in the interests of seriousness I had had to run all the way from the door of St Stephen's right into his room. After this, when I burst as though across the tape into his office, he merely raised his eyebrows slightly, and, smiling, continued whatever he happened to be doing.

But the anxiety of the two friendly policemen was more than matched by the hostility of the head clerk. This poor man, it seemed, had actually invented the job I held, telling Sir Patrick when he first became Attorney-General that it was impossible for his existing staff to take on the extra work, that a new secretary was needed, and all this on account of a poor niece of his own who badly needed the money. So, when Sir Patrick accepted the proposition but gave the job to me, the poor man's chagrin was naturally very great. He never showed this openly to me, and I might not have been aware of it had he not repeatedly made complaints of my behaviour and my work to Sir Patrick, who, aware of his motives, repeated his remarks as a joke to my father. Then one day he apparently determined to take stronger action. Coming into the office where I was idling about reading a book, he gave me a long envelope containing some papers.

"Sir Patrick is at No. 10 Downing Street at a Cabinet Meeting," he said, "but this is a matter he must know about at once. So you'd better go there and take these papers to him."

Nothing loth I put on my coat, went out and hailed a taxi. I was interested to see the inside of No. 10 and pleased with the importance of my job, and so when I arrived at my destination I rang the bell without any fear and asked the butler quite boldly to bring Sir Patrick Hastings to me. Two or three minutes later, when Uncle Pat himself arrived, I merely thrust the envelope into his hand and told him that the clerk had told me to bring it. Then I went off and thought no more about the matter. But during the next day or two I came in for a great deal of petting, and finally I was told, again by my father, that the papers had been of no importance, and that the only thing which excused my extraordinary mistake in sending for the Attorney-General in the middle of a Cabinet Meeting was that the Attorney-General himself had recognised the malign hand behind my behaviour. I was not very much disturbed, because I could never see the point either of the clerk's action or of the petting. It seemed to me that I had received an instruction from an obvious superior and carried it out, and that neither blame nor affectionate commiseration could well attach to me. And now that I know more about the society in which we lived, I find it odd that no one was ashamed that I should play about in this job while the poor clerk's niece was out of work.

However, all this was soon to come to an end, because Sir Patrick Hastings himself, by instituting proceedings against Mr J. R. Campbell, editor of the *Worker's Weekly,* an antecedent of the *Daily Worker,* under the Incitement to Mutiny Act of 1795, and by later withdrawing the proceedings, brought about the fall of the first Labour Government; and he and I together lost our jobs in the House of Commons.

This did not matter very much to me because the job had never been more than a cover for my real occupations, which, as by a small gesture was later to become apparent, took place in a night-club. The only part of my day that was in any way affected was that between four and six o'clock in the afternoon, because it had long been established that Miss Chesher, my father's secretary, rather than listen to me thumping a typewriter in the mornings, would do this part of my daily task for me.

I am unable to this day to explain to myself why it gave my father so much pleasure at this time to take me about with him. The society we frequented was composed entirely of his own friends, and, although they were often much younger than he was, they were equivalently older than me. In almost every sense my continual presence beside him was quite out of place. If he had been a doting and uncritical parent who admired all my actions, it would be easier to understand. But he was far from that. One of the simplest divisions of the human race it is possible to make is into those to whom the fact of possession gives the transforming power of love, and those for whom it renders everything suspect. There are people for whom a quite ordinary view of the countryside becomes truly magnificent when seen from a window of their own room, and others for whom such beauties as there may be, seen from this position, are forever obscured by a small factory chimney in the far corner of their vision. My father belonged neurotically, obsessively, to the second category. His exceptional confidence in himself gave way to a white heat of tortured disloyalty when he felt socially responsible for anyone else. In the biography I wrote of him I endeavoured to explain his attitude to England in the last war, an attitude which made him very unpopular in America. In a letter to me written on the publication of the book, a friend of his developed the point I was trying to make with a phrase I wish I had thought of myself.

"As a matter of fact," she said, "I never heard it suggested

67

that he was pro-German, but he was apt to shout 'Britain's done, finished, my dear fellow,' and as you say, people didn't like it . . . I think he said these things as an insurance, just as he said over and over again down the years 'I have cancer, I'm done, darling!' or as the Chinese say 'My odious son!'"

My odious son. . . . Never, during the whole of my youth, did my father introduce me to a room full of people without presenting me, in effect, as 'My odious child.' If I had on a dress which I had lately bought but which was a little bit gay or daring, and which I wore hopefully but with qualms, he would say: "My daughter, who for some reason of her own has decided tonight to wear fancy dress." If the dress was quiet and plain, he would remark: "My daughter, who, in spite of the enormous allowance I give her, has decided to spend none of it on clothes." Having thus effected my introduction to a group of people, terrifyingly old, smart, beautiful and famous, he would hurry as fast as he could to the other side of the room, so as not to hear and suffer from the foolish, hesitant replies that, thus dashed, I would make to any conversation addressed to me. If, during the dinner that followed, I spoke at all, he would cover for me with ridicule; if I did not speak he complained to my mother next morning that she had given birth to a litter of idiots. Ridicule is of all weapons the most annihilating to the very young, and I cannot imagine how, in spite of his addiction to this type of insurance, I managed so much to enjoy myself. Perhaps it was not, as I thought then, pure loss. Perhaps people were kinder and more sympathetic to me because of my perpetual humiliation, and, consequently, quicker to make friends. In any case, when he called to me in the evening to dress and come out to dinner, I never hesitated to do so.

The night-club where I afterwards usually found myself was called the Embassy Club, and, since to my memory it presents a microcosm of the life of whole sections of the society of the time, I think it is worth some description.

The swing doors at the entrance to the restaurant opened on to the long side of a well-proportioned room. All round the walls above the sofas and the tables looking-glasses reflected the scene. The whole of the centre of the room was a dance-floor, but late at night when the restaurant was full, and almost always at luncheon, tables placed uncomfortably close together would edge towards the middle of the room, until there was almost no space left in the centre. At one end of the room, on a balcony above the floor, was the bandstand. In the course of a few years the restaurant was several times re-decorated, but it was always dignified and subdued, unmistakably designed to receive only the very rich.

The dominant figure in the room, one of the period pieces of London, was Luigi, the manager. A man with a proud and ascetic head, grey hair and a grey moustache, he had, when he chose, a royal manner—an imperturbable memory for faces, a gracious and well chosen word for old favourites, an assured and flattering familiarity with the famous. He must have been un-usually competent. It was said that in the Embassy Club one could get anything from a Player's cigarette (an uncommon requirement for those days) to a white elephant within three minutes of asking for it. But the thing that sticks chiefly in the mind about Luigi was his incredible arrogance with the general run of his customers.

In a restaurant that is crowded and popular, only a small percentage of the customers can have the best tables. In Luigi's restaurant quite a high proportion of his clientele had to be perched on small chairs in conditions of overcrowding that, for sheer weight of human flesh to the square foot, would have com-pared unfavourably with that later achieved in a concentration camp. Peace had to be preserved somehow. Luigi preserved it, with the most terrifying insolence, by treating his customers like lackeys.

This technique is difficult now to understand. In logic it would be reasonable to assume that the warm and caressing manner, the jokes and the flattery might have gone in recompense to those who, denied the spacious sofa-tables, sat huddled together, unable to hear themselves speak, in the middle of the floor. But this was never so; and night after night people fought each other for the last remaining tables.

Man, the psychologists tell us, is a self-injuring beast, smoking fifty cigarettes a day without receiving pleasure from one of them, prone to self-inflicted accidents, gloatingly enduring self-made tortures. Perhaps in certain phases of society he also finds it necessary to pay extremely high sums to be publicly humiliated.

Either that, or Luigi was right, and his customers were for the most part lackeys. For, every now and then, when his restaurant was emptied by some other passing fashion, he would single out one or two of his less distinguished customers for the treatment usually accorded only to the stars. And possibly then the pleasure imparted, the showing-off permitted, was great enough to bring back these poor, humble fish again and again, in the hope that the promotion was genuine and not the result of a passing whim. In any case, there is no doubt that men who had spent the whole day harassing their employees, who had boasted to their wives in the bath, came night after night to the Embassy Club to have the smile wiped off their faces by Luigi.

And the inhuman arrogance of this well-paid bully caused no comment either from those who received it or from those who watched it, because it was a characteristic of the age. To this day, when a saleswoman in a woman's fashion shop is portrayed on the stage or in a caricature, she is shown as walking with mincing steps on very high heels, looking from half-closed eyes down a supercilious nose, and addressing her customer as "Moddom." But it is years since any saleswoman has behaved in this fashion, and the picture is derived from the time when Luigi presided at the Embassy, and the first job of a saleswoman, attending a customer come to buy an expensive dress, was to put the fear of God into her.

The second figure of importance at the Embassy was Ambrose, the band-leader. He earned his money in the mornings, one must suppose, in organisation and rehearsals of the band. In the evenings he stood on the balcony, violin in one hand, bow hanging down from the other, leaning inertly against the piano, looking down on the throng that circled gradually round below him. And, as he thus surveyed his patrons, the look of weariness on his rather good-looking face deepened, as his eyes went out of focus, into one of ever-greater boredom and contempt. Two or three times during the evening he would pull himself together and play a chorus on his violin, but soon he would lapse again into silent contemplation, leaving the dance-music to his well-trained band. He was much beloved, and, if his air of uncon-querable boredom might elsewhere have been regarded as a shade impertinent, it was such a gentle, melancholic thing beside the gem-like edge of Luigi's manner, that here it passed for a sad disability for life.

To this room night after night for years the fashionable society of London came, and it seemed that the dancing we had known in Birchington had been nothing but a seaside try-out for the scene which filled every suitable room in London. In the Embassy were dukes and earls and princes and their wives and the women they loved, writers, actors, press-lords, politicians, all the self-made men from the war who were trying to break into society, all the riff-raff and the hangers-on. At home in the great houses in which these people still lived there were cooks and kitchen-maids waiting to cook a dinner, butlers and footmen waiting to serve it. But their masters and mistresses at the Embassy Club sat at their tables only until the waiters served the soup, and then, as though mechanically activated, they all got up and began to dance. In this restaurant one could eat as well as any-where in the world, but the food was always crammed down between dances, drowned with gin-and-tonic, blown over by cigarette-smoke.

At dinner-time, and most people dined late at about nine o'clock, the room would be reasonably filled. In was later, after the theatre, that the tables were jammed together over almost every available inch of floor. Early in the evening, when the whole room could be seen with a relatively unimpeded vision, it would have been possible for an acute observer to watch the rules of an older society gradually being broken down. For the

71

first time in history the British upper classes were opening their ranks and allowing wholesale ingress to rich men, famous men or women, notorieties, anyone who could add a scrap to their entertainment. And very largely it was this that was causing the crush and the excitement, this that made Luigi's tyrannical rule a possibility. At the Embassy the clientele that Luigi favoured all knew each other, and met there as in their own drawing-rooms. With the nodding and waving and calling out and transferring to one another's table that went on there, the opportunities for social climbing from outside this group were unequalled. And for people by whom no actual gain could be recorded, there would always be splendid opportunities for showing off.

"There's old So-and-So," one might say, waving and smiling, and intercepting a wave intended for someone else. And:

"You don't remember me, but we met last night at the Embassy."

In the early years, when I was seventeen and went there with my father, a good deal of zest was put into all these pursuits, and the society there seemed to me infinitely exciting and glamorous. There were the great hostesses of London and all the beauties—Lady Cunard, sitting most nights with Sir Robert and Lady Abdy; Mrs Richard Norton and Lady Louis Mountbatten, Miss Paula Gellibrand, later to become the Marchesa de Casa Maury, whom many people thought the greatest beauty of them all, Lady Loughborough and Miss Poppy Baring, Miss Tallulah Bankhead on her very best behaviour, and many another male and female star from the theatre. Sometimes, too, there would be seen amongst the dancers a small fair young man with delicate pouches under his eyes and the mouth of a sulky waif. When he was there Luigi's manner became exceedingly royal, grave and impressively courteous. In the Embassy Club I saw, too, the last of the courtesans, the last of the women who lived professionally and solely on the wealth of a rich benefactor. A tall, blonde young woman, she always wore the most beautiful clothes, a reflection, it was said, of the great taste of her patron.

These women had never been made welcome in society, and I heard Lady Cunard, who has been so much idealised by her friends since her death as to have become unrecognisable, but whose greatest gift in her lifetime was a wittily inconsequential turn of speech, which, never aimed directly at nails, often succeeded in tapping them a neat, passing blow on the head, say of this one:

"I said to her: 'You should go on the stage, my dear. Then we could all know you.'"

But this was the morality of an older generation—you may do what you like, but not openly and not professionally—as this young woman was to prove, by not going on the stage and by marrying the son of a peer. And she was the last of her tribe because it was no longer necessary to pay for these things.

But as the years went on and the first fine flush of irresponsibility went out of it, this life at the Embassy became simply a habit, a habit that no one could break. And this is incomprehensible. For these people were not all young—the prices were far too high for the very young—nor were they all idle or silly. Less and less were they there to make love to each other or even, with any real skill or enjoyment, to dance. Most nights the small space left for the dancers was so crowded it was impossible to do more than stand jigging slightly in one place, and in the rooms where the floor-space was bigger or the popularity less, much of the dancing was done by men of middle age who, holding their partners ungracefully and at length, shuffled round the room out of time. It was merely the way people lived, a tic that had grown upon them during the chaotic years after the war, and which now they were unable to conquer.

Largely it was the women who forced the pace. Certainly many a tired stockbroker or busy professional man sat in a crowded, noisy and smoke-filled room night after night until about two o'clock in the morning, because it was his only opportunity, a broken and restless opportunity, of spending any time with his wife. But it was not all or only the women. I can remember when an unmarried man of well over fifty became

Chancellor of the Exchequer—probably the ambition of his lifetime—he received and accepted a certain amount of commiseration because it was now considered undignified for him to be seen very often in a night-club. And people had become so used to living their lives in public that they had lost the habit of privacy. Probably the oddest phenomena of all were the pairs of lovers, their relationship well known to everyone, who night after night sat dotted around the sofa-tables, their backs to the wall, seldom dancing, having long ago exhausted the art of conversing with each other, watching the floor until the early hours of the morning, their eyes, like Ambrose's, absent and glazed. What stimulus, one wondered even then, induced them to forsake all privacy for this weary watching and waiting?

As I have been writing these words in an attempt to capture that scene of long ago, a conviction has been growing in my mind that this has been done before by an enormously popular writer of those days. Memory is such a provoking thing. So often when I have the opportunity to confirm or deny mine, I find that there is no basis whatever for a version of some event which lives in my mind as though it had taken place yesterday. So I have grown constantly more uneasy, and, as I wrote the last word, I went to the bookshelf and took down a book. Turning over the leaves I found the place quite easily, and here, after I have with the use of dots excised a certain verbosity, is what I read. Allowing for the mannerisms of this author, which in the space of only a few years earned him one of the biggest fortunes ever made by a writer, but in almost as short a time caused the great British public to be unable to read one single word that he wrote, I know not whether to be more pleased at the confirmation he gives to my memories, or more chagrined by the undoubted deftness with which he does it.

"The Loyalty [Club] sprang from the Embassy and it sprang in a polite direction, from Bond Street down the hill of St James's to Pall Mall, where it might lie over against Carlton House Terrace. It sprang because certain persons of *ton* had found that the Mother Society, while never ordered but with the most polite amenities, was growing perhaps just a little crowded with what-nots; had, by banding themselves in a body financial and social, founded the Loyalty; and were there assured of more freedom for the exercise of a reasonable exclusiveness since, the floor-space of the Loyalty being large enough to accommodate only one hundred and fifty dancers, the membership was strictly limited to one thousand and five hundred."

I think that Michael Arlen denied that he was writing about the Embassy Club itself, not from any desire to give a passing nod to the law of libel, but so as to draw his reader's attention to the fact that it *was* the Embassy he was about to portray; also because he liked the joke about the one thousand five hundred dancers; and thirdly because he had a passion for making things move down the hill of St James's.

"The Loyalty Club can, however, claim no historical notice but in the person of the Chevalier Giulio di Risotto, its *directeur du restaurant* . . . A study of the lives of philosophers and statesmen will inform and ennoble the mind; but a sideways glance at such a phenomenon as the twentieth-century Risotto cannot help but make it supple. One of the menials of all time, he is one of the successes of ours; and a portent of the doom of aristocracy in England. Born of Machiavelli by Demoiselle Demi-monde, crafty, thin, pale, dry-shiny as shagreen, he had walked to fortune about every great restaurant in Europe, adding always, but with great discrimination, to his order of *l'aristocratie internationale;* . . . The 'creation' of the Loyalty Club must serve his biographers as the pinnacle of Risotto's career . . ."

Of Ambrose, he says this:

"Astorias, *chef d'orchestre,* stood at rest by the edge of the balcony, his violin under his arm, his bow gently tapping the edge of a bowl of nameless ferns that hid his feet. His negligence is informed with depression, his poise leans on melancholy. The Blues, that man knows. He seems to wonder why he is there, why anyone is there. . . . No one can tell him, so he goes on doing nothing, lonely as a star in hell. He does not toil, nor spin, nor play his violin."

75

Before leaving the Embassy Club and Michael Arlen, I am going to take one more quotation from his book because it is highly relevant to the life I was leading at the time.

"Nearby," he says, "was a corner-table of eight young people. Maybe they would dance later on. Suddenly one of the girls would give a loud laugh, and then there would be silence. Of the four young men one looked as Richard of Gloucester might possibly have looked, a little bent, a little sinister and pale, as though he had been reading a treatise on diseases far into the night before. They were four married couples, and they had all been boys and girls together, and they had a son and daughter apiece, and they all went to the same dentist. The women had white oval faces, small breasts, blue eyes, thin arms, no expression, no blood; literally, of course, not genealogically. One of them stared with wide blue eyes right into people's faces, and blinked vaguely. She was lovely . . . Presently, a prince of the blood joined them, there was a little stir for a minute or two, a little laughter, and then he rose to dance with the girl of the blind blue eyes. As she danced she stared thoughtfully at the glass dome of the ceiling. She looked bored with boredom."

At the time that he wrote these words Mr Arlen knew none of these people, and the details of the son and daughter apiece and the dentist, although probably correct, were his own invention. He must have sat near this party in the Embassy and watched them, for the two characters he describes, the Richard of Gloucester and the girl of the blind blue eyes, are instantly recognisable to anyone who knew them, and since, not long after this and for several years, they were to be a part of my own life, I shall return to them.

But first, to complete this picture of any ordinary evening in society in London, I must explain that, although the Embassy was a club, and to enter it one had either to be or accompany a member, in every other way it conformed to the standards of a restaurant or hotel ballroom. The night-clubs proper, to which people went much later in the evening, were not so very different from the few that exist today. The chief differences were in the numbers—there were dozens all over London—in the clientele, and in the amount of attention they received from the police. Then it was the habit for all the middle-aged people as well as the young married couples from the Embassy to pass on to one of these night-clubs at about one o'clock in the morning; and there, having earlier ruined a five-course dinner by dancing right through it, to fill themselves with bacon and eggs and lager beer, preparatory to sleeping through half the next day. The attention of the police was occasioned by their interest in the drink laws. Almost as much ingenuity went into circumventing the letter of these laws as is now exercised on the laws relating to income tax. The police often raided these night-clubs, but on these occasions they were constantly presented with new and legally innocent evasions of the spirit of the laws. At one time nearly every night-club in London presented the appearance of a large private bottle party, the drink having been bought at some other time and stored until it was required. The entrance to these clubs was usually in some small dark mews, and in an office immediately inside it sat the man responsible for seeing that at least the letter of the current method of evasion was kept. This occasioned continual rows, because the rules changed from time to time, and people, arriving with large parties in gay mood, resented being held up and made to comply with the latest one. One hardly ever passed in except through a number of people wrangling at the entrance.

A journey in a lift or down shoddy stone steps would land one in some ill-lit cave, where occasionally there might be a band of real talent, and life ground on into the later hours of the morning. These places must have been only fitfully profitable, for fashion swept into them for a few weeks, and out again soon for no predictable reason. But there was also a slightly different kind of night-club which had a more enduring life. These were the ones run by the bohemians of London for themselves. Here there would be cubist decorations on the walls, and the young man in the high-necked sweater serving behind the bar might easily be some temporarily out-of-work actor. I think that these were open at lunchtime too and had a life which continued throughout almost the whole of the twenty-four hours. In those days, when theatres began at 8.30 and did not finish until after 11, almost all the acting profession ate late at night, and this provided a continuous clientele for the places of their choice, as well as a draw for the rest of the world to come and view them.

The rules of society did not permit young ladies of a higher social position than mine inside any of these places, but I attended them night after night, drinking nothing stronger than orangeade, and thrived very well on it, driving home when the water-carts were out washing the streets of London.

6

BEFORE I can describe more of my life at this time, I must make an attempt to re-create the atmosphere in which young girls lived.

I have already suggested that this was a pushing, competitive society, in which old rules were being broken and new ones yet scarcely formulated. This lack of standards, of known patterns of behaviour, created an irresponsibility that was touched to a truly wanton triviality by the easy money made during the war and in the post-war boom.

"Every time we thought we might make one pound we made five," a stockbroker said to me once, "and every time we hoped to make a hundred we made a thousand."

This creates the attitude of the gambler towards spending: "I can make or lose more than this on the first race, so who cares?"

But if it was a world of great opportunity, it was also one of great fears. Competitiveness breeds anxiety, and, when most things can be bought with money earned without effort, there is a vulgarising of human values that is paid for by instability and, in the end, by boredom and disillusion.

In the first place everything was curiously stereotyped. Only one type of female beauty was admitted. I have quoted Michael Arlen's description of a party of young women at the Embassy Club: "The women had white oval faces, small breasts, blue eyes, thin arms, no expression, no blood." This will serve for a description of the pattern to which all women who hoped for success in society had to conform. Girls, not naturally born to it, had, by means which nowadays seem as unreasonable and artificial as the Chinese binding of feet, to be forced into it. No man could love a fat girl, but, more than that, no man could love a girl who exhibited the blooming plumpness of youth. Girls not endued with flat breasts and boyish figures were dieted constantly at home, and, if this was not successful, they were put into a nursing home and forcibly thinned. I know of at least two young women who died in their early thirties from diseases brought on by constant dieting in their teens.

Skirts were worn extremely short, and to be born with fat legs or thick ankles was an innate disaster like being born with a hare-lip. Girls with large breasts (which today might make their fortune) had them strapped down until the ligaments were broken and they hung disconsolately, like those of an elderly negress, to their waists. Hair was cut short, and although I conformed without much trouble to the figure required at the time, I was constantly vexed by having normally pink cheeks. I admired so much more the effect, achieved on a white face, of rouge applied high on the cheek-bones.

Women's clothes, too, were all of one pattern, the pattern of the French couturiers. To be well dressed was to be dressed by one of the great French dressmakers or by one of their hundreds of imitators. This is not to say, as every male novelist throughout the ages has believed, that the hallmark of elegance was a simplicity so quiet and expensive as to be unnoticeable. On the contrary, then as now, the greater the art of the dressmaker the more daringly and unexpectedly he might sometimes apply it to colour and to cut. But since no imprint, no departure from the style of clothes that were portrayed in such magazines as *Vogue* was conceivable for those who wished to conform to the standards of fashionable London, it was largely to be forced into these that girls' figures had to be starved and cut about to one pattern.

This excessive desire to conform physically to one type was certainly no odder than the one that produced the wasp-waists and sloping shoulders of earlier generations, but it was much more widespread. The Great War had killed two million men, creating an abnormal shortage of males, but the break-up of society was offering the middle classes opportunities in the marriage market which touched to hysteria their natural class-consciousness.

Much harder the running, but much greater the possible prize.

The parents of daughters, and this applied equally to the threatened upper class, were obsessed with anxiety as to their future. For girls, completely uneducated and unable even to run a house, only one successful outcome could be visualised; and with a shortage of men, life for young women and their parents took on the aspect of a tournament in which only by keeping fit, obeying the rules and constantly knocking out one's opponents could one hope to win the prize.

Love and a natural desire for the happiness of one's children played some part in the attitude of the parents, but pride and the desire for self-glorification through one's offspring, which had embittered the relations of successive generations for hundreds of years, was conspicuous too. No shame, no disgrace more painful than to possess an ageing and unmarried daughter (in the higher spheres no outcome so dull as a younger son); no victory so rewarding, no pleasure so great as to marry her well. Unfortunately there were other shames; old, prurient, unnatural shames, left-overs from the morality of the Victorians and their primly ridiculous beliefs about the proper attitude of a woman to a man which had to be guarded against. For the first time girls were beginning to go about without chaperones and to enjoy a freedom unknown in the past. There was considerable uneasiness about them. I have described how, in my own family, the desire of my parents to see their three daughters married was equalled by my father's neurotic fears about our virginal state. In the upper classes this fear, more dignified and more controlled, nevertheless expressed itself in a desire that young ladies should not "make themselves cheap." When a girl, who had been brought up to believe that her sole job in life was to be attractive to men, attempted to be so, she was immediately warned against the dangers of "making herself cheap"—a scalding phrase to anyone of the least sensitivity.

The girls of the day reacted in one of two ways. Thinned down, taught not to show-off, required to be spontaneously charming, told to attract the young men, reproved for doing so, the high spirited ones kicked right over the traces, set out to scandalise the older society and to find a new morality. Ultimately they began to believe they had found this in a gallant and negligent disregard of caution, in unshockability and a desire to shock. Also they boasted a good deal. Human nature remaining much the same in most essentials, they did not cast away their virginity with the ease they would have had it thought, and their adventures were far more of a noisy, adolescent kind—schoolchildren baiting their teachers—than as deeply and cynically incautious as they made believe. The society they were to form as they grew up was satirised by Evelyn Waugh, but he had a personal ruthlessness, a true contempt for the world, to which most of his models were merely pretending.

Nevertheless, in spite of the triviality of its expression there was, in the youth of this generation, seldom referred to and faced only in the lonely hours of the spirit, but erupting again and again in its literature, a romantic despair, a destructive discontent. And, while a few of the bolder spirits cut loose from the inhibiting influence of their parents, far more of the girls of the time were destroyed by it. Young men, who were there only to be married but with whom contact could so easily produce this cheapening effect, became as dangerous and as untouchable as rattlesnakes. Again and again my contemporaries have said to me: "You see, I was so terribly shy in my youth, because one felt that if one spoke to a young man he would immediately assume that one wanted to marry him," and the more analytical have added: "And even by not speaking, one could still not avoid his knowing that in fact, of course, one did."

As a result, many of my contemporaries married the first man who asked them, so as to get into harbour, and many more, retiring ever further into themselves, either have not married at all, or have married late, when youth, with its pleasures and its fears, was over. The terrors of those days account, too, for the fact that so many of my female contemporaries are unnaturally dull. When people cannot be themselves, they acquire a front behind which to retire from the world. This is apt to be conventional and stereotyped, and, if worn long enough, tends to become the whole personality, smothering all original impulse or thought.

The ideas that governed the behaviour of our parents were not new and have died hard. (Nowadays, when I and my contemporaries watch with such pleasure our daughters—a surprising number of whom have thick, or thin but unshapely legs—gambolling like puppies with groups of their contemporaries of both sexes, those of the grandmothers who are present to witness the scene still hiss into our ears: "It's all very well. But is anyone *serious*?") These ideas are inevitable in a class society, where the girls are not educated, but they became exaggeratedly felt in the circumstances of my time.

Further symptoms of uneasiness were the arrogant manners, not confined to Luigi or to shop-girls, which one so often met. Almost everyone was arrogant to someone. In theory it was not considered the act of a gentleman to be rude to servants or waiters, but I often heard it said of someone that it was unpleasant to go out with him because of his manner to waiters—which is inconceivable today. Debutantes were arrogant to other debutantes, carrying on with the giggling and affected discourtesy of their schoolrooms towards anyone they did not know. Eligible and unattached young men were arrogant to almost everyone. I, in common with many another of my more nervous contemporaries, was merely arrogant to women of my mother's age. I knew that they feared me, and I knew that this fear was inspired by the fact that my skin was firm, while theirs was veined and beginning to wrinkle, and my eyes were clear while theirs were bloodshot; and, since I regarded this as an immutably fixed relationship, I felt that by now they ought to have found other causes for pride, some acceptance of their horrible fate. And in a sense I was right. I was never arrogant to Miss Marie Tempest who was far older than they were, nor to Miss Gladys Cooper, younger in fact, but not in my eyes. On the contrary, I was very timorous with both of them. But nor was I arrogant to Miss Chesher, my father's secretary, no wit, no beauty, but no

83

craven hanger-on to youth. It was the competitiveness, the determination to keep in the swim that made possible the arrogance.

But by now I was beginning to make myself tiresome to my mother in many ways. For my father and I had gone into society.

As a girl I belonged by nature not to the hardy, trace-kicking spirits, but to the sufferers. But although I suffered deeply in the presence of young men, I suffered very seldom, since I scarcely ever met one.

I knew Mr E. V. Lucas, who once gave me a five-pound piece that had belonged to his mother, which I carried about me for luck, until I lost it one day in the hunting-field, to my everlasting regret. I knew Mr Rudolf Besier, and I own a signed copy of *The Barretts of Wimpole Street*. I knew Mr Arnold Bennett, who regularly at first nights in London asked me my opinion of the play, and always appeared to be interested in my answer. I knew Mr A. E. W. Mason, and, sitting next to him one night at dinner, I told him that, after observation and reflection, I had come to the conclusion that marital love was an invention of novelists, which shocked him so much that he spent the rest of dinner in an attempt to change my opinion. I knew Lord Beaverbrook, who made the only serious contribution to my education ever made by anyone. I knew Mr Ronald Squire, who coached me at tennis on a hard-court at Golders Green. Above all, I knew all the young married couples and all their lovers in the high society in which my father spent most of his time. Once, it is true, staying with a school-friend I met two young men in the navy. But, when I asked them to our house, my father, pulling at his nose as he observed them, frightened them so much that they seldom came again. And indeed I had no ambition to ask them, because the recognisable if faintly cagey air of ridicule in his manner when he said to me afterwards: "Charming, your friends. Charming fellows!" was, above all else, the thing in the world from which I suffered most.

But at this time I cared little for the deprivation, because I was in love with the high society, the young married couples who were giving a demonstration of how very attractive human nature can be when all the circumstances are propitious. And since, although no one was yet aware of it, this was about all they were doing, it deserves some attention.

My father took me one night to dinner in a private house where there were six other people. The first thing I noticed was the astonishing beauty of the women. This was no accident. In those days the upper classes were apt to be better looking than other groups of people, and, since they were not geneticists, they themselves believed this had something to do with the blueness of their blood. There were two reasons for it. One lay entirely in the art of hairdressers, dressmakers, dentists, physical training instructors and cosmetic-makers. But the second reason, and by far the more important, was that beauty is not only skin-deep. A beautiful woman, from the time she is a child, attracts attention, and this gives her confidence, the greatest fertiliser of all. Wit and intelligence, or what passes for wit and intelligence, are often merely the result of this confidence—ease in society and audacity—but, since they are very successful, they give a shine to the eyes and a bloom to the cheeks, a carriage to the head and a dash to the walk. If you start, as the upper classes did, with an absolute certainty of superiority, if you are spoilt by the servants and schoolmistresses, by the neighbours, and by your father's guests and tenants, it is surprising what it can do for the looks. The rule holds throughout. In the hunting-field it was not the leathery-faced countrywoman who led the field, but some hunting-capped lightweight from London. The girl who drove the ball straight down the fairway off the first tee was the one who had been up until five o'clock in a night-club. Today in any big hairdresser's shop in London it is possible to pick out three or four girls, manicuring the nails or holding the pins, who are as intrinsically beautiful as the three women at dinner that night, but, looking at their delicate heads, one wonders whether the slightly over-painted, mask-like, little faces are the same in all circumstances, or whether, in the evening with the boy-friend, they light up a little and gain genuine charm. It takes more than good features, a little money and a lot of artifice to make real beauty.

That night I knew none of this, and I was enchanted. The men were impressive too, if only for the wonderful cut of their clothes, their extreme ease, and their flat gold cigarette-cases. Humanity was much improved in those days by the habit of dressing for dinner, and much pleasure is lost in this scruffy age of duffle-coats and mackintoshes. Before dinner everyone drank martinis, not the gin barely scented with French vermouth of today, but a vile concoction of equal parts of gin, French and Italian vermouth. They played records on the gramophone that they had brought from America—Al Jolson singing "California Here I Come" and Cliff Edwards singing "I Know I'm Losing You," and my heart beat with the rapturous despair of youth.

At dinner at least two of the men were genuinely witty, and the women unexpected. They were in the process of inventing the phrases which have lingered on the lips of debutantes and suchlike ever since. "I couldn't like it more," "I couldn't care less." Everyone chain-smoked throughout the meal, and, although this is a disgusting habit, it then seemed to me very dashing. Everyone called everyone else darling, and at least one of the women used the language of a navvy, the word bloody peppering her conversation as it peppered my father's. Since she was the most beautiful of them all, and to me the most glamorous, try as I will and in all the most unsuitable circumstances, to this day this word keeps popping up in my own conversation. My youngest daughter, lately reproved at school for saying she could not tie "her blasted shoe-lace," replied: "Well, if you don't like blasted, you ought to hear Mummy." But that night these two unattractive habits did represent originality and freedom from convention, which were both quite new to me.

But it was when we left the dining room and as we walked up the stairs that I first fell in love with these people. Life for me is always illumined in flashes. Just as I know whether I like someone or not, not so much by his considered conversation as by the undertones of an afterthought or the reply to an unexpected question, so the horizon of my mind is constantly widened, not by the nobility of discourse, but by a single sentence. Walking up the stairs that night, one of the women said to another:

"This is the dress I bought in Paris. Do you like it?"

And the other replied:

"Well, I would if it wasn't for that tarty bit of ribbon round the neck."

That was all. For me it opened up a whole new plane of thought and behaviour.

If one of my mother's friends had been asked that question, she would have replied: "Yes, I think it's simply lovely," but, thus inhibited, later she would have been extraordinarily vicious about the piece of ribbon to some third person. There was a good reason for this. My mother and her friends would have had only one or two new evening dresses in a year. It would have been thought impossible in their society to criticise a dress which must perforce be worn on many subsequent occasions, but the mealy-mouthed convention of speech which their circumstances forced on them made for back-biting and suspicion. The women I was with that night had ten or twelve new dresses at a time, and, in any case, the one wearing the criticised dress would go back now to the dressmaker and say: "You see, darling, I can't wear it with this tarty piece of ribbon round the neck," and he would alter it for her. I saw only that the essence of good conversation, the basis of friendship, the large, the fine, the unusual thing, is truth.

And, in fact, if the circumstances of my sudden understanding were so insignificant that the incident is difficult to explain, the discovery itself was not nothing. If truth were so common, it would not be so highly valued, the confident classes would lose their peculiar power to charm, and good conversation would not be so rare. Intellectual circles have always understood the necessity, but intellectuals are so often neurotic that somewhere a weakness will show itself (all too often, even today, related to the class structure), sooner or later a moment will arrive when language ceases to communicate intention. And for me, and I am convinced for many other people, the fascination of the British upper classes has not been their wealth or their rank, but the ability these have given them to stand the truth. It is from this that all their attractiveness follows.

And so, for several years, I followed this little group, mimicking their behaviour, listening to their intonations, copying their clothes. And never a young man except those attached to the young married women.

This, and particularly this little section of it, was a doomed society. It could not be said that they were fighting a rearguard action, because they were not fighting at all. They were sailing along on a fast-ebbing tide, enjoying the excitement. They still had this belief in their own superiority, and, although they no longer showed this unless seriously scratched, it blinded their eyes to the shape of things to come. It was based almost entirely on things that do not bear a moment's objective examination. First, there were all the shibboleths, such things as that nowadays known as U-speech. When the upper classes say "I am going to London," they feel some superiority over the man who says: "I am going to town," in spite of the fact that their grandfathers said: "I am going to town," while the commoner said: "I am going to London." They notice that some people say "lounge," or even "parlour," and in the most pedantic circles they apparently notice "mantelpiece." When I drive my very fast car to London these days, I am amused to find that I cannot control a feeling of superiority towards the drivers of all the cars that I pass on my way. Possibly, if I had had a fast car all my life, and if I was one of the very few people who had one, I should not be aware that my feeling is funny. And even this is not an exact analogy, because my car is in fact faster than most and was earned with the sweat of my brow; it is not merely that I have arranged with myself to think it faster.

These are small and unimportant things, but if one doubts that they represent a quite serious feeling, one only has to turn to the openly expressed opinions of a generation earlier than the one of which I speak. Lady Emily Lutyens is still alive, and her contemporaries were the mothers of my friends. Here are some extracts from a letter, published in *A Blessed Girl*, which she wrote when she was eighteen, describing a charity ball given in London.

"There was not a single soul in the room that we any of us knew . . . There were the most wonderful collection of people I have ever seen, and their costumes [costume is a word which, I think I am right in saying, is no longer U] were more wonderful than themselves. The dresses are going back to early Victorian fashion, and it really looked like the old ballrooms of fifty years ago. The people were very smart and there were a great many hideous and bright colours, heliotrope prevailing of a shade that took the skin off one's eyes. The people were all of a class which you would never meet anywhere else. They seemed to be all strangers to each other, and there was occasionally a couple seated on the same sofa looking miserable and not saying a word."

To which her correspondent Whitworth Elwin replied:

"You are accumulating experiences. I can picture the fun the ball must have been to you. The company were probably a compound of affectation and nature. They meant to be artificial— that is, highly fashionable—but their lesson had been imperfectly learnt, and nature, stronger than their efforts, kept breaking through. . . . Lucky you to be mothered by Betty. My Lady would not have taken you to the ball. . . ."

Now at a charity ball given in London in 1893 there is really no doubt that the heliotrope-covered savages were the British upper-middle classes. But this is no surprise to anyone who, seven pages earlier, has read of Mr Asquith.

"He is not quite a gentleman, which is very much against him."

And indeed the English class-structure was terraced like a vineyard, each considering himself a gentleman, and lumping all the strata he considered beneath him together as "not quite." In my day this upper-class consciousness of belonging to a different and superior order was almost equally strongly, although far less obtrusively, felt. Because of it they seldom questioned their innate understanding of how to behave in all circumstances. And yet, at their worst, they have always been capable of degrees of vulgarity unknown among those to whom they feel so superior. There are people who think that, although Lady Emily Lutyens's letter was written in all innocence, it was a trifle vulgar to publish it. In any case, it is safe to assume that, if she had belonged to any other class, the upper-class reader would have taken the view that she had done so not from a personal idiosyncrasy, but because she came from a sphere where standards in these matters were not very high. But this is disputable territory. Almost everyone would agree however that it shows a defective sense of behaviour to push to the head of the queue, to call out to other people in high voices in public places, to use rank and position openly to achieve what one wants at the expense of other people. These are all things that few of the people I knew in my youth would have had any hesitation in doing. My father and I once sat at a table in the Ambassadeurs Restaurant in Cannes with a peeress of the realm. Presently she sent for the head waiter and told him to ask the little negro singing with the band to sing some particular song. In accordance with the custom of those days, when he sang it he wended his way through the crowd, and, standing beside our table, sang it to the lady herself. But by then she was deep in some conversation which interested her more, and, during the time that he stood there, she never showed by the blink of an eyelash that she was aware of his presence, nor did she make any attempt to thank him when his performance was over. For her, the whim of the moment being forgotten, he did not exist.

In London during the nineteen-twenties it was well known to hostesses anxious to have lions at their tables that every man had his price. For one it might be the presence of some other particular lion, for another a high fee paid to a visiting Italian singer might do it, for a third the expectation of meeting some beautiful woman was enough. Only find out the particular weakness, and the most retiring, the most determinedly exclusive, would succumb. It was left to an American hostess called Mrs Corrigan to discover that the price of all that was noblest and most aristocratic in London society was gold cigarette-cases and jewelled bracelets. Mrs Corrigan, having arrived in England determined to conquer London, experienced some difficulty. Her very eagerness was against her, and, although her parties were from the beginning well attended, they had not what Michael Arlen would have called *ton*. More than that, by rushing too fast at her fences, she had managed to set up a resistance. Then she hit upon the idea at one of her parties of giving an expensive present to each of her guests. After this, for a price that was probably no higher than one of her compatriots would have paid for an Old Master, she had, with one or two honourable exceptions, the whole of London at her feet.

When I was seventeen I actually liked the vulgarity as well as the superiority. Trampling on other people, calling excitedly to my friends, I felt I was one with them. Their technique was to sweep you over to their side of the barrier by discussing everyone else openly in your presence. Some years later, when I was staying in a big country house, my hostess said to me:

"Today we have to give a middle-class luncheon party, so you must behave yourself."

To my amazement the guests at luncheon were the inhabitants of the smaller manor houses of the neighbourhood, what are known as the gentry, people who, in other circumstances, might not have known my mother or myself. Without difficulty, however, I swallowed my surprise, and condescended to behave myself.

But by then I was aware of the absurdity of the position, because quite early in my life I had been taught a short, sharp lesson in the realities. It happened that the eldest son of a baronet fell in love with my sister and wished to marry her. The fuss that the baronet made was only equalled by the meekness with which the whole of my family accepted it. We were not especially meek by nature. It was simply that the class-boundaries were still so well defined that we accepted the rights of the baronet as we would have accepted the rights of the King. I, however, never forgot it, not because it rankled, but because it was a practical guide as to what to expect.

When I was seventeen the special friends of my father and myself were the two people described by Michael Arlen, the Richard of Gloucester and his wife, the girl of the blind blue eyes. This foursome, the young man and his wife, my father and myself, could be seen night after night at the Embassy Club, or some other place of its kind, sometimes with others, sometimes alone. And this had an ugly look to certain sections of society, who began to murmur against it. When the rumour of what was being said reached the ears of my poor father and mother, they nearly died of fright. So for several weeks I was incarcerated at home. It was then I tried for the first time the power of melancholy, which my sister had been using so successfully ever since she was fifteen. My father and mother were always defenceless against us for this reason—they believed that it was necessary to keep our confidence so as to be able to influence us in the crises of life. But during the crises of life they were so afraid that a strong stand would lose our confidence that, except in the most tentative manner, they were unable to influence us.

"Leave her alone," they used to warn each other. "Leave her alone, or she'll never tell you anything again."

Everyone holds something particular against their parents. I hold this. When one is very young and threatening unorthodox behaviour, half the time one is hoping to get one's face saved by being forbidden it. Our poor faces were never saved the smallest blush, and often we were forced to prolong situations for which in truth we had little heart.

But on this occasion my heart was in it, and I mooned round the house, white-faced and silent, until, in a very short time, and after receiving assurances from me on several points, my parents capitulated, and I returned once more to the night-life.

We used to play golf too. I know by heart all the golf-courses round London, and often we would stay a week-end at Birchington so as to play on the courses at Sandwich. I was spoiled extremely, and taught to take a high hand about everything.

92

But this friendship did not last forever and after a year or so we drifted away into other spheres.

I think it was when I was eighteen that my father took me to a house in Fulham, because we were going to play golf with Lord Beaverbrook. I have said that Lord Beaverbrook made the only valuable contribution to my education ever made by anyone. This was how it came about.

It is well known that Lord Beaverbrook has a natural talent for cross-examination which enables him to find out almost everything he wishes to know. What is not so well-known, perhaps, is that he is also a natural schoolmaster. I speak with all modesty when I say that he must have stretched the first of these talents to the full when he discovered that deep in my heart there was locked a desire to write. Maybe I should in any case have had a reverence for the art, but I had been brought up to believe that this is a talent denied to all but the very few, and that nothing but the most terrifying and unnatural arrogance could suggest that one might have it. Once, when my mother repeated to my father in my presence that one of my schoolmistresses had said that I had a style, he turned on her and me:

"Get that idea out of your head," he said to me. "These women know nothing about such things."

There were, I think, three reasons for his attitude. The first was honourable. He had himself a great respect for the art of writing, and he believed it should not be smeared by the un-talented. The second reason was "my odious child." He was not prepared to let any of us risk anything that, if not well done, would make a fool of him. He expected us to be highly successful, much liked, and to marry well; but he expected us to do all this with an unobtrusiveness which could never bring shame on his own head. The third reason was again honourable. He knew well that his name then stood so high that any of us could sell under it things which would never have been bought on their merits. And he was not prepared to let us do it. Since he could never take up any attitude except in the most violent way, and since I, no less than my two sisters, was terrified of his lightest word, I cannot imagine how Lord Beaverbrook succeeded in dragging my secret out of me. However, when he did, he gave me two pieces of advice. Both had great and continuing results, but of a different kind.

He told me first that, as a preparation for my future career, I should study the style of successful practitioners of the art, and, by attempting to imitate them, achieve the technique of writing. He proposed an exercise. I was to write, he suggested, an article for him three times, each in the style of a different writer; one, he insisted, must be Kinglake (and he gave me *Eothen*), the other two I could choose for myself. I do not think this was good advice for me. I know that this method was followed in his youth by at least one writer of great talent, but for those with little gift it seems to me to have dangers. I have forgotten the second writer I chose, but the third was Michael Arlen; and, whereas I was able to catch his mannerisms sufficiently well for him, when he afterwards read my article without knowing the circumstances in which it had been written, to tell my sister that I had plagiarised his style, I was completely unable to comprehend and consequently to imitate the more classical structure of Kinglake's sentences.

Michael Arlen read my article in the following circumstances. Lord Beaverbrook, always unpredictable, when he received my three effusions, returned two of them heavily criticised, but the third, the Michael Arlen, he published under my name in the *Daily Express*, without word to anyone.

However, in attempting to help me on in my career, he had reckoned without my father. The scene over this incident took place at breakfast, and, since Lord Beaverbrook had not confided his intentions to me, for some time I was unable to discover its cause. My father's tongue had the lacerating power of a cat-o'-nine-tails. On the occasion that words of mine first appeared in print, he used it to such effect that all ambition to write lay pulverised in my heart for twelve years.

However, the second piece of advice Lord Beaverbrook gave me had much more enjoyable results. As a child I had always been a voracious reader, with that power of concentration which excludes from the mind the noise of a whole roomful of people. But I do not know what I read. Of the classics, I certainly read *Alice in Wonderland* and *Through the Looking-Glass* when I was very young indeed; at about the same period or soon after I read *Little Women* and the whole of the series that follows it. I read *The Jungle Book,* and *The Three Musketeers* and *The Count of Monte Cristo.* But with these exceptions, I feel certain that I am right in saying that none of the masterpieces of literature ever came my way. At the schools I attended there were no libraries, and no guidance was ever given me in literary taste. At home I feel convinced that from the youngest age I read the novels that my mother got for herself from the local lending library. I can remember that when I was about eleven I asked her what the word "seduced" meant, as I was unable to follow the meaning of the book I was reading. She replied, with what she considered great adroitness, that if one was induced to leave someone, say one's doctor or one's lawyer, and go to another, one could be said to have been "seduced away." So indeed one could, but, on returning to my book, I came to the conclusion that she could not understand the meaning of the word herself, and, since there was no dictionary in our house, I learned the habit of judging the meaning of words by the sense in their context they conveyed to me, a habit which has led at times to some strange mistakes on my part. But when I was eighteen Lord Beaverbrook earned my undying gratitude by telling me that, if I wished to form a literary taste, I must for one whole year refuse to read anything but the great works of literature, after which, he assured me, I would find it difficult ever again to read anything else. This is the kind of advice I can accept with enthusiasm, because, being in my own way a perfectionist, I love absolute rules; and the year began at the moment of his uttering the remark.

I do not remember all that I read in that year; Lord Beaverbrook himself contributed, in addition to *Eothen, The Life of Jesus* by Renan and *The History of England* by J. A. Froude, and, under the influence of Michael Arlen, I read a great many translations—almost the whole of Dostoievsky, and *Anna Karenina*, the first six volumes of Proust, these being the only ones yet translated, *Madame Bovary*, and much of Anatole France; but I kept to the rule absolutely, with results not so far from those Lord Beaverbrook had predicted.

The extent of my reading was enlarged by the fact that the days when I trotted all over London with my father were now ended. For some time there had been trouble in our house. My father was beginning, in reality, to leave my mother, from whom he was never divorced or legally separated, but with whom he never again shared a house. There was much unhappiness between them, and this was greatly exacerbated by his habit of taking me with him into his new life from which she was excluded. She believed that her worry was entirely for me, and, indeed, in the view of many people, she had grounds for concern at the company I kept. For months she quarrelled and argued with my father, and perhaps her words began to take effect, but the *coup de grâce* was given by someone else. Late one night at some party Miss Fay Compton said to my father:

"Freddy, that girl ought not to be here."

That finished it. I was returned, at any rate for the moment, to my mother's care.

7

I WAS born with an enthusiasm which, if I am to be happy, has to be kept at full stretch. On the whole it has made my life enjoyable, but, at times when I can find nothing to extend it, it reduces me to depths of discontent and depression. Fortunately for me it is a stupid thing, easily fobbed off. For months at a time it can be kept quiet by some such exercise as an attempt to reduce my handicap at golf from eighteen to fourteen. For years it was completely satisfied while I tried to breed a high-class herd of Ayrshire cows. Life is always agreeable when I am learning something. Anything will do—dressmaking, cooking, an attempt to manipulate a Leica camera—but whatever it is must be done with a single-minded intensity of purpose.

In the closing months of my nineteenth year I was lonely, bored and eaten by discontent. The atmosphere in our home was uneasy. My mother and father quarrelled incessantly, and when they were united it was in gloom at the realisation that nobody was getting married. My elder sister was not yet twenty and I was eighteen, but to my mother and father our grown-up life seemed to have dragged on uselessly without even a step in the right direction. They were weighed down by consciousness of their failure as parents. They had no method of launching us.

For the middle classes this was always a difficulty. The season of the upper classes, which from afar has always appeared to be slightly ridiculous, did have the merit of providing young women with an enormous circle of friends, some proper basis of choice. But because the middle classes could not afford this extravagant introduction into society, their children were confined to the company of their neighbours, the sons and daughters of business friends, or people met on holiday or by some other accident. Since none of these could be entertained regularly or in the lavish way of the upper classes, horizons were small.

All these difficulties were accentuated by my father. Egotistical to the last degree, he knew everyone he wanted to know, but his restless, unconventional and still youthful nature made any kind of circle in which young girls could be adequately presented to the world an impossibility. My mother knew very few people, but, in any case, on the few occasions when she attempted to give a party for us, my father's critical presence ruined it. He could not endure the unfledged youth of the middle classes.

They did everything they could to make up for this. We each had an allowance of £250 a year, with which we had nothing to do but dress and amuse ourselves. We also had a car, originally an old AC belonging to my father, but later a new Morris Oxford. Every now and then we were taken abroad. This was partly because my father was extremely generous and wished to give us all he could. But it was always decided upon when the marriage-hysteria reached some crisis. My father and mother both had this pathetic belief that if one changed one's surroundings it could only be for the better. Because of it they for years moved their house in London about once every six months, and because of it the atmosphere of hope before we were taken on a holiday foredoomed it to failure. We were always taken to the obvious places, usually on the French Riviera, and here, if in fact we met anyone at all, it was always the people we already knew in London. And my sister and I, knowing that the object was to bring home a young man, had our permanent sense of humiliation and ineptitude heightened to a point that made me believe, until about ten years ago, that I hated travel.

On the Riviera I merely exchanged the golf professional in Regent's Park for the professional on the hotel tennis court, and my sister, less ambitious, went shopping with my mother. We both exchanged the night-clubs of London for those of Cannes. We usually had some friend of my father's with us. On one occasion at least it was Michael Arlen, for I remember him practising his golf-swing in the hotel sitting-room, and also his replying, when my father reproved him for spitting on the carpet as he talked: "That is astral manure."

When I was seventeen my father took my sister and myself to America, and when I was eighteen he took me again by myself. These visits were the most oppressive failures of the lot. All the way over on the *Olympic* or the *Majestic* we danced every evening, but almost entirely with quite old men; arrived in New York we could not even dance. This was at the time of prohibition, and, at the kind of parties to which my father took us, by ten o'clock in the evening everyone was so drunk that we had to be sent home to bed. So we went to the theatre night after night alone together, and, after three or four weeks, were weeping to go home. When I went alone it was better, for my father and I were always amused by each other's company, and he could not send me to the theatre by myself.

It was now that I began to pay quite heavily, however, for his preference for me. He had more money than he needed, he worked very seldom, although very fast when he did, and he was beginning to throw off all responsibilities as a married man. He began the ceaseless wandering round the world which continued until his death, and which was really a kind of madness. He was always looking for a place where he could be happy and where he would find it possible to write. He made extensive plans to go somewhere for a period of six weeks or so, but arrived at his destination he began to fidget within a day or two and returned home within two or three. At this time, when he had decided to go to Birchington, or Jersey, or the New Forest, he always wanted me to go with him. The rest of my family were determined I should go. When he was at home he interfered with their plans, made their friends uncomfortable, seriously spoiled their lives, and they hoped that, if I accompanied him, he might stay longer away. For me whole worlds of boredom and discontent opened at the thought of the hotel bedroom, the dreary meals while he talked either of his play or fretted about whether we should stay or go. I knew that the penance would never be for very long, but,

99

until we had actually embarked on the journey home, there was always the fear that this time he would change his ways. The first night in any of these places he would be very happy and gay and talk of the play he was going to write. This was very hard to endure. One had usually heard all about the play a dozen times before, but one was expected to laugh at the jokes and exclaim at the twists in the plot as though one was an audience in a theatre hearing it all for the first time. The fact that he was so happy was also depressing. One could never believe that in a matter of hours his mood would change completely. The next morning we would play golf, and, if he played well, at luncheon he would still be quite gay. But, before night fell, one knew that release was in sight. It always began with an attempt to reassure himself. Everything would be extravagantly praised.

"How good the food is in this hotel," or "We must go and see old So-and-So. He is a most charming fellow, and you'll like him very much," or "Miss Lonsdale, this is the place to live. I think I shall buy a house here. It may not be very gay or amusing, but it is better than talking to all those perishers in London."

Soon after this he would have a very long telephone call with his doctor in London, or his agent, or the manager who was going to put on his next play. One of these three would, before the end of the conversation, somehow be edged into saying he thought it a great pity my father was not in London, and my father would, with many protestations about the miseries and difficulties of a life in which nobody would leave one in peace in a pleasant place where it was possible to work, decide that he had better go back. It is not easy to be sure what went on in his mind, but I think that these conversations were not primarily for the purpose of fooling me. He was often dishonest with other people, but nearly always, I think, with himself.

I would not have minded these wearisome journeys so much if he had not invariably chosen the times when there was something amusing going on at home, which I consequently missed.

And not much that was amusing happened at home at this time. Except for the golf-lessons and the reading I had nothing to do, nothing that I had ever done seemed to have led anywhere, and I was shattered by boredom and frustration. After some months of this I decided to get a job. Since I was entirely uneducated and untrained, and jobs were very difficult to get, I tried for the only thing I could think of.

I had heard that Constance Collier and Ivor Novello were about to put on a new play in which there was a part for a young girl. I telephoned to Ivor, whom I had known since I was a child, and asked him if I could see him. Presently I found myself in a studio-room alone with him and Miss Collier. I explained that I wanted the job.

"Take off your hat," Ivor said, "and go and stand with your back to the piano."

I did this and received the full light from the window in my face. I stood there, rather self-conscious and terrified of what they might ask for next, until, after some minutes, Ivor spoke again.

"What do you think?" he said to Miss Collier.

"I think she might do," she replied.

Not much more than five minutes later I found myself in the street, to my amazement having apparently landed a job in a new London production.

My father was lunching at home that day. When I explained rather excitedly to my family that I was about to go on the stage, he was unusually quiet, although he made me tell him in detail what had happened at the interview.

After the meal was over he went out of the room, re-appearing again about ten minutes later.

"Your job's off," he said curtly.

"What do you mean?" I asked.

"I have just spoken to Ivor, and I told him that if he gave you this job, neither he nor Constance would ever get a play of mine as long as I live."

Then he raised an admonitory finger and wagged it at me.

"If you want to go on the stage," he said, "you can do what anyone else would have to do, and get a job on tour."

I am not sure whether I had the sense to be glad. I do know that I had no illusions about my ability as an actress, and that when I had gone to see Ivor I had not seriously believed that anything would come of it. But it has always seemed to be one of the disappointments of life, a chance missed, and it is only now, thinking back on it, that I realise I took it all very quietly, and probably it was the one occasion in his life when my father really fulfilled the proper function of a parent. However, at the time I was sufficiently angry to go and see Mr Barry O'Brien that very afternoon. Before evening I had landed my second job of the day, a small part in a first-class tour of my father's play *The Last of Mrs Cheyney*.

I was quite pleased with the outcome. It might be amusing to go on tour. Then I heard that Ronald Squire, who was acting in the play in London, was going to produce the touring company. This was bad, but worse was to follow. Ronnie had recently privately coached Miss Margaret Bannerman to a triumph in *Our Betters*. Flushed with this success, he now offered to do the same thing for me. I was appalled. I knew perfectly well that I had absolutely no talent as an actress, but I had thought that in the quiet world of a touring production I would somehow get by. I had known Ronnie for years, and he had a sense of humour and power of ridicule second only to my father himself. I had often roared with laughter at his imitations of some actor or actress of professional competence with whom he happened to be playing or whose performance he had witnessed, which always ended in a burlesqued and half-comic scream of anger:

"The fool! He doesn't see that . . ."

The idea of being privately coached in our own drawing-room reduced me to such a shivering mass of self-consciousness that I could hardly open my mouth. The part that I had was a small but very good one. More than that, intellectually I knew exactly how it should be played. I understood my father's dialogue, and this part had been based on the girl with blind eyes at the

Embassy Club, of whom I had been giving a living imitation for several years. Finally, after much perseverance, Ronnie gave it up.

"We'll see how you are at rehearsals," he said.

But after the first rehearsal he came round to see me, and told me that I should have to change with Doris Cooper who had been engaged to play a much smaller and entirely dreary part. I made it as difficult as I could for him, because I wept, but this was more from chagrin at my own stupidity than from anything he had done.

We toured all round the first-class towns and I enjoyed it very much. When my friends were in front I was always a source of great pleasure, because I made up so badly that I looked about forty, and I had very few speaking lines, of which one was:

"I am a good woman."

In the north-country towns we stayed in theatrical lodgings and for supper ate tripe and onions, a dish to which I have been devoted ever since. In one of these towns I had an odd experience. As I was rushing late into the stage-door one night, a man stepped out of the shadows of a wall and spoke to me.

"Are you Miss Lonsdale?" he asked.

When I said that I was, he said that he was my uncle, my father's brother. I explained that I could not wait and implored him to agree to some arrangement to meet. But he flatly refused. He had decided years before that it was unsuitable for him, in his position, to know my father in his, and he did not intend to alter his decision. He had not been able to resist the opportunity simply to look at me. I had never seen him before and I never saw him again. The truth is our family has a devilish spiritual pride.

When we came south I fell in love with a dark-haired undergraduate in Oxford who had a passion for the opera *Louise* which he played on the gramophone. He was the first intellectual young man I had ever met. But he was very detached, and he scarcely noticed me.

In Birmingham I got the only notice from a dramatic critic I

103

was ever to have. He said that I could not walk and was not as good as I thought I was.

"The question is," I wondered, "how good do I think I am?"

And it was while I was still on tour, but at home for a week-end, that something happened which was to change the whole course of my life. There arrived quite late one evening at our house an Alsatian puppy in a basket addressed to me. There was a ticket inside which said that his name was Buff, but otherwise no indication of where he had come from or why he had been sent. Much later I found out that he was a present from someone who wished to give him to me, but who, having lately had a fierce quarrel with my father, was afraid that if it was known who had sent him, I would not be allowed to keep him. At the time the mystery added greatly to the puppy's already considerable charm. After this I induced my sister to let me take our jointly shared car on tour and Buff went everywhere with me, beloved of landladies, in spite of certain messes, and adored by me.

But it was at the moment of my greatest triumph as an actress that enlightenment as to the futility of my adopting this profession came to me. In the week that we played at Golders Green, the whole of the London company from the St James's Theatre came to the matinée to see our performance. On this very day Zena Dare who played Mrs Cheyney got flu, and Doris Cooper, understudying for her, moved into her place, while I moved into the part I had originally been engaged for. I have said that I understood better probably than anyone else exactly how this part should be played. By this time I was used to the stage, and could make my voice heard in the farthest corners of the enormous theatres in which we had to play. Fired by the presence of the whole London company, I gave the only inspired performance of my career, and all the grand company from London came round to congratulate me, including Gladys Cooper herself. Nevertheless, something had happened on the stage which could not be seen from in front.

There was a moment in the play when I had to come on to the stage pealing with laughter. At the rehearsal of the understudies in the morning, I had proved quite unable to do this. I opened my mouth again and again but nothing came. In the end I arranged with all the female members of the caste to stand in the wings and roar with laughter, so that when I went on to the stage, doubled up but perfectly silent, it would not be apparent to the audience.

I knew that the moment had come to rest on my laurels. It was quite clear that I could not for the rest of my life persuade every-one in the company to laugh in the wings whenever I had to laugh on the stage. And apart from this, what, I wondered, was going to happen if the day should come when I was required to cry?

I did not confide my intentions to anyone, but when I was offered the better small part in a second tour, I stipulated that I should be allowed to understudy Mrs Cheyney, which con-sidering my age, apart from any other disadvantages, was an impossible request. And so, with more honour than I deserved, I retired from the stage.

By then I had certain plans for Buff. He was a very charming and exceptionally intelligent puppy, and it was not merely that I loved him; my enthusiasm had fastened upon him. He was going to be a dog with a future. In the first place I had decided to have him trained in police work so that he could run in Field Trials (he did, in fact, become a Field Trial Champion several times over), and secondly he was going to have a wife. To bring all this about, however, I had somehow to persuade my mother and sisters that they wanted to live in the country. This task was made easier by my sister, who had formed a sentimental attach-ment for a gentleman horse-dealer a few years older than my father, which was driving my parents to distraction, but which they had not the courage to stop. She said that we would not merely live in the country and breed dogs, we would also take up hunting. As a preparation for this we went round every morning to Horace Smith's riding school to learn how to ride. The gentleman horse-dealer advised us to learn side-saddle, as he said it would take too long to become very proficient astride. My mother's opposition to the whole scheme was unexpectedly weak, because she was by now finding it impossible to share a house with my father, and, besides, any excuse was always good enough for her to move house.

We started our country life in a small Tudor cottage near Crawley, which my father had bought for himself. But, on the only night he spent there, he had been so lonely he had passed the evening in the kitchen talking to the servants. We did not like it either, because it did not suit our hunting plans. So in no time it was sold again.

We moved then to a white house on the first slope of the downs at Alfriston. It was a house with a curious history, because it had been built by Horatio Bottomley and sold by him to Clarence Hatry. When someone made the joke, "Built by Bottomley, sold to Hatry and lived in by Frederick Lonsdale," my father thought it merely unfunny. The house had an enormous range of horse-boxes, and Bottomley's horses had been trained on the downs above us. We filled four or five of these boxes, some with our dogs and their puppies, and two with horses, one for my sister and one for myself.

My sister had a horse that was apparently much nicer than mine. He was a very smart chestnut and, when he reared up as straight as a young larch tree on the downs, we were so ignorant that we thought it was because she could not ride. It was only after he had thrown everyone else who rode him, including, I am glad to say, the gentleman horse-dealer, off onto the ground as soon as they got on his back that it was realised that he actually loved my sister and behaved far better with her than with anyone else. I had an extremely uncomfortable old bay mare who had seen far better days, and I was conscious of having been rather badly fobbed off. However, I did not seriously mind. It was so heavenly on the downs, and every day we exercised ourselves and our horses, and fed our dogs in the most scientific way. But we had difficulty over the hunting, because my mother was convinced it was too dangerous and that we did not yet ride well enough.

It was then that we met the local Master of Hounds at some luncheon party, and I sat next to him and explained our difficulties. He said that he would persuade my mother to let me go out with his second horseman, who would look after me. We had no idea what this meant, but my mother rather nervously agreed, and, with much excitement and tying of stocks, I went off to the meet.

The job of a second horseman is, by knowing the country, to keep near the hounds as they run, so that in the middle of the day his master can exchange horses, but never to tire or heat the horse, and, as far as possible, never to get off the road. I understood his job immediately, and was completely dissatisfied. So I waited, trotting along on the roads, which is excessively tiring and uncomfortable on a side-saddle, until the groom went home with the first horse. Then I fell in behind the field, aware that, since no one knew who I was, no one was likely to stop me.

This was a very easy hunting country, mainly a question of jumping the local Sussex heave-gates and small fences, and galloping about in the woods. The old bay mare turned out, in an unambitious way, to know her stuff. When the hounds checked at the end of the day, flushed, exhausted and plastered with mud, I jumped the last post-and-rails with a slight crash behind four or five other people.

After this even the dogs were neglected. We insisted on having two more horses bought for us, so that we could hunt three days a week, and when we were not hunting we were grooming or exercising our horses. For six months we were blissfully happy, boredom a thing of the past. There was no way of telling that all this was to be my undoing.

It was in the following year, and largely as a result of the life we were leading, that my mother forced me, by the maximum of pressure, but also with extraordinary duplicity in the strangest set of circumstances, to marry a man twenty years older than myself, whom I did not want to marry.

I am not very easily forced, and I do not think that she could have succeeded except that, although my father was in America, I counted absolutely on the belief that when he came home he would regard the whole thing as utterly ridiculous and stop it at once.

However, I misjudged him. When he arrived, he circled round the situation, suspicious, and with the manner of a dog who has just seen a ghost. He talked at length to my mother, but he did not talk to me. Then he left again for America. It is only fair to say that he knew nothing of the circumstances of my engagement.

On the night before the wedding, when the presents were laid out in a room below, and, since it was a country wedding, some of the guests were already on their way, he came into my bedroom at midnight.

"Look here," he said, "you don't have to do this, if by any chance you don't want to. There's still time to get out of it."

My father was a very complex character, but very transparent. I can remember no time in my life when I did not understand him better than anyone else did. I have spoken often of his unique charm, and his gay and affectionate nature—also of his enormous egotism. The quality in him that was finally irresistible was that he was an unhappy man, and seemed so vulnerable—expectant and eager, but foredoomed, a man without understanding. Because of this quality, I loved him with a fierce and protective love all his life.

On this night, when he came into by bedroom at the eleventh hour, it was obvious what he wanted me to do. He wanted me to insist; to give him the assurance, now and forever, that he had had no part in this marriage, that whatever might happen in the future it was no fault of his. And so I gave it to him.

The behaviour of my parents was not in fact different from that of dozens of families, who ought to have known better, when an eldest son or a rich man appeared on the scene. What, in my parents' case, was a little pathetic, was that there was no need to set their sights so low. Legally I had to have their permission for this marriage, because I was under twenty-one. But my father was the talented son of a Jersey tobacconist, putting up a wonderful show, and my mother was a daughter of the great middle classes who had never had the opportunity to learn anything. Their income, although at this time enormous, was entirely precarious. They succumbed to their fears.

8

FOUR years after the events I have described I was free and back in London. The obstructions to my having achieved this sooner were all in my own mind, and they were all entirely irrational. Since I have a firm reputation among people who know me for a practical and logical turn of thought and behaviour, I am going to attempt to describe exactly what went on in my mind at that time.

During the first few months of my marriage it became clear to me that, as I had already suspected, I had got myself into a purposeless and life-wrecking mess. I was able to bear this position with equanimity because, during the whole of my life, I have had the superstitious notion that, while all may not necessarily be for the best in the best of all possible worlds, there is a benevolent fate interested in me. Whenever things go wrong for me, I am always buoyed up by the thought that it is probably all for the best, that when I am able to look back from the vantage-point of ten years hence, I shall be able to see that, if I had been given what I wanted at this particular time, it would have stood in the way of my getting something far better later. This preposterous theory has gained great support in my mind from the facts of my two marriages. I have been very happy and well suited in my second marriage, and I have since believed that, if it had not been for the first one and its extreme misfortune, I might not have waited long enough, might not have been free at the moment of opportunity.

The second reason why I was not unbearably unhappy in this first marriage is that I was armed with a conviction that sooner or later without effort on my part I should get out of it.

There was nothing concrete to prevent my doing this immediately I realised that the marriage was, in all senses that I can think of, unreal. But I thought it would be disorderly to do so until a certain amount of time had passed. A good deal of trouble had been taken and some tribulation endured to get me married. Nothing could be gained by becoming immediately unmarried. The decorous period of time seemed to me to be about four years. I always assumed, when I thought about it, that I would be free before my twenty-fifth birthday.

This arbitrary number of years became fixed in my mind quite early, certainly in the first month or two. The fact that I kept to it almost exactly and was never tempted to shorten it was due to my fear of public opinion. Since, of all the thoughts and emotions by which I was controlled, this operated in the most nonsensical way, I am going to make what may appear a digression so as to illustrate it.

In the summer months when I was not hunting I used to go to take riding lessons with a horse-dealer at Redhill, named Sam Marsh. He was considered by many good judges to be the finest all-round horseman in England, and he was a talented teacher. During these summers he often mounted me on one of his horses in the show-ring. One year he owned an exceptionally beautiful chestnut called Scamperdale, a horse with an unpleasant history. He had twice run away with women in the show-ring. On the first of these occasions he had been ridden by a woman very well known in the show-world, and she had screamed, so that the incident was well known and remembered. He had then been sold locally in Sussex and the performance had been repeated, although, I think, without the screams.

Sam Marsh had been forced to take the horse back, and only chance now of selling him well was to win so often and so sensationally with him that his previous reputation would be forgiven. Sam determined to ride him himself all that summer.

One day I received a telephone message to go immediately to a small show I had not intended to go to, and to be prepared to ride. Arrived there, I found Sam Marsh seated outside the ring with a broken leg stretched out in front of him, and Scamperdale being led up and down. Sam said that I was to ride the horse, and he gave me short but exact instructions.

"Get on top," he said, "and don't breathe."

This, to those who understand the parlance, simply means that one must keep as quiet as one can and never interfere with the horse at all.

I always find it difficult to take responsibility because I am too anxious. This is a thing that only I understand about myself, because I have on occasion appeared to be taking far more responsibility than is normally held by a woman. On these occasions, however, there has always been someone in the background whom I have regarded as the ultimate authority, and to whom I have been able to defer. This person's word is, for me, in the sphere of his authority, law; and it is the fact of this law behind me that enables me imperturbably to assume a position that without it is alien to my nature. Sam Marsh was, at this time and in all matters connected with horses, the law. Never could I have been persuaded to attempt to ride Scamperdale unless he had told me to do so; but after I had heard what he had to say, I waited for the groom to put my saddle on the horse, and then I got up on his back. Outside the ring I walked, trotted and then cantered him. Every now and then he raked at the bit with nervous impatience, pulling his head and neck forward. When he did this I dropped my hands and let him do it, otherwise I occupied myself trying not to breathe. When I wanted him to stop, I dropped my hands while heading for some trees, and he pulled himself up. I was conscious that there was one factor that might make success in the ring itself possible. It had not rained for weeks and weeks, and the going was so hard we should not be asked to gallop. When a horse is asked only to canter collectedly and quietly about, he never gets excited. If this horse had been asked to gallop, his hot blood would have made my orders inadequate.

When I got into the ring I simply obeyed these orders, and, except for dropping my hands when Scamperdale raked at the bit, I did nothing. After we had walked, trotted and cantered round the ring for some time it became necessary to pull up. I still did nothing, but, as the other horses gradually slowed to a standstill, Scamperdale pulled up too. For weeks and weeks of that summer it did not rain, and for weeks and weeks I gave the same performance on Scamperdale, always winning first prize. I had only one difficulty. After winning one is supposed to lead the other horses once round the ring, the rosette held in one's teeth. I could not lead round the ring, because, once in front, I should finally have had to pull the horse up. So I always had to fiddle with a stirrup-leather or the bridle until the second prize-winner in exasperation led off in front of me.

In the show-ring, after the judges have pulled in the first half-dozen or so of the horses they prefer, they ride each one of them in turn. When the judges got on Scamperdale, they had first of all to turn him away from the other horses, and then they had to try him out thoroughly, cantering him about and pulling him up whether he was willing or unwilling. They all soon discovered that he was a bad-tempered devil and a terrifying ride. As I had ridden him without blinking an eyelash, they none of them could admit their own difficulties, otherwise they might have put him down a place or two in spite of his exceptional conformation. (I have always wondered since at Sam Marsh's hardihood. If I had lost my confidence for one second and annoyed the horse, I should immediately have sailed off round the ring as had my two predecessors, and when this happens it is a horrifying experience for the onlookers as well as for the person concerned. I was once run away with in the show-ring on another horse, one with a perfectly good temper, but too strong for me. After I had had time to decide that I was never going to be able to pull him up, I turned him out of the ring and rode him straight at the stables that stood behind it. When we got near them he propped as hard as he could on his front legs and stopped, and I jumped off. This took only the smallest confidence, because no horse is going to gallop straight into a wooden wall, nor—if by chance the half-doors should be open—is he going to gallop straight inside his stable. I rode with such enthusiasm but so little experience that I had more than once had to practise a manoeuvre of this sort at home. So, when I dismounted, I was still in perfectly good trim, but everyone else was shocked and trembling with fear.)

Because of the apparent perfection of my horsemanship on Scamperdale, I earned a great deal of admiration from the judges. One of these was a fat old man who was the Master of Hounds of one of the two packs with which we used to hunt, a courteous, kind and respected old man, and a consummate horseman. When he congratulated me on the way I had ridden the horse, I tried to explain that the whole thing was a fraud, and to tell him the secret of my unexpected prowess, but he would not listen long enough to understand. After this he always gave me a special welcome out hunting, always smiled at me whenever he saw me, and obviously admired me. That was really all; I do not remember ever going to a meal in his house. But when the time drew near for me to leave my husband, I was seriously held back by the thought of this old man. I thought the break-up of my marriage might shock him, and I quite strongly did not want to lose his good opinion. I cannot remember whether in some compartment of my mind I realised that he was unlikely to be interested for more than a few minutes in any behaviour of mine, and was still unable to control my instinctive fears, or whether my feeling was so subjective that I believed his shock would be a real one. I only know that immediately before and when I left Sussex, my unhappiness at the thought of this old man was genuine and strong, and that emotions such as this sustained me during the whole of my self-imposed residence there. Three days after I had left this place I had, of course, forgotten them all.

But the thing that above all else made these four years a possibility is that I have a capacity for enjoyment. In the literature of the twentieth century I am always astounded to find that this is something that is never taken into account. In novel after novel the whole of life is treated as a matter for despair or for a kind of satirical stoicism. All human beings are represented as ludicrous, inept, squalid and unsuccessful, all personal relationships as cold and unreciprocal, tragically thwarted if not actually humiliating, all hopes are treated as a subject for comedy and all fears exploited meticulously—the world a vale of tears which differs from novel to novel only in the matter of whether over the whole there is a glaze of actual insanity, or merely of an unselfpitied but accepted drabness. Is it, I sometimes wonder, that the great gifts of these authors are balanced by a melancholy temperament which colours all life to their view? Or is it that I am exceptional? Because I enjoy myself almost all the time, and, not only that, I nearly always feel myself to be successful in anything I seriously undertake. As I look round at my neighbours, I fancy I observe other people who are equally happy in their married lives, enthusiastic over their pursuits, heedlessly joyous a great deal of their time. Above all, they do not seem to me to have, as I certainly have not, the self-knowledge, the awareness which, in novels, turns every aspiration to ashes. But how can I tell? Perhaps it is I who am mad in a sane but accursed world.

In any case, nearly always in my life I have been able to find something to enjoy. During these four years I enjoyed the horses and the dogs. I usually had two or three horses and they were always brilliant. What makes a good horse is first of all make and shape and quality, but in the final resort he must be willing, eager and brave. And these are qualities it is impossible not to love. Particularly are they lovable in a small horse, as all mine were, whose ears seem permanently cocked at fences almost as high as himself. The first horse I had was a bay named Top Rail. He was slow and rather uncomfortable, but, without any assistance from me, he would collect himself and jump a clear foot over the top of any obstacle that came in his way; and he would do this if every other horse in the hunt had refused it in front of him. Later, when I was considered to ride a little better, I had a grey mare called Smoke, a blood mare called Bally Girl and a brown gelding called Long Island. The first two were aged and well schooled, but the third was too green for me, and I have it on my conscience that I spoiled him. Later, however, he belonged

115

to someone more adept who turned him into a splendid hunter.

A lot has been written about hunting, but much of it is without knowledge. It is too late now to set out to defend the hunting of the fox, but what can be defended is the attitude of the people who take part in it. This is not, as is so often believed, in the least sadistic, although it may be completely callous. Country people have a necessary callousness which is not understood by townsfolk. Anyone who has ever seen a fox pause and look about him as he crosses a ride in a wood in front of the hounds, knows full well that his fear is not nearly so great as is that of a sheep every time the shepherd catches him to trim his feet or inject him against some disease. A sheep is cornered and caught often in his life, and whenever this happens he suffers the extreme of hysterical fear. Every time his fear is quite irrational except the last time; and then he is right, because he is on his way to the butcher. When a pig is killed he is caught and held, and a vein in his throat is cut, so that he shall bleed slowly to death to make a meal for animal-lovers. And all the time he is dying he screams, a harsh and blood-curdling scream, that everyone on the farm dislikes to hear. He is not screaming because he is dying a slow and tragic death, but because he is being held; just as, when a lamb has his tail cut off, he never notices the pain, but suffers torture because he is picked up. And the pig and the sheep and rabbits disturbed playing in a hollow in the evening sun seem to experience a fear unknown to the fox, who is wily and brave, except in the last extremity, when, of course, one does not know. But death comes to everyone in the end.

And the attitude of the countryman to all these things is that he hardly thinks about them at all. He lives with them, and if he felt as emotionally as the people who write to the newspapers, he and they would both starve. Many farmers who breed beef-cattle regard these animals with such pleasure that they have a picked bunch in the field in front of their bedroom window, so that they may see them while shaving. And they will spend hours leaning over a gate admiring their points and their health. But

116

the time when they look at them with the greatest happiness is when they have just made top price of the day to the butcher, after years when they have been almost as much a part of the family as the dogs. Nevertheless, countrymen are seldom sadistic, and they will sit up much of the night to save an animal unnecessary pain, or to keep life in the body of one lamb that has suffered exposure to the weather; and if one wants a litter of kittens drowned on a farm, it is quite likely that one cannot find a single man to do it, which accounts for the fact that so many farms are overrun with cats. And all this seems to me admirable and healthy, and in any case necessary; moreover, it is an attitude which makes fox-hunting possible without the extreme of barbaric emotion which townspeople think they detect. For the fox is as necessary to a scheme of things as is the poor pig bleeding to death; and if we could live without fox-hunting, so indeed could we live without pork.

The reason why the fox is necessary is that when a drag-line is laid for the hounds to trail it is not, as is so often suggested, the same thing as a wild animal who runs where he wills. A drag-line must be laid by a man, and a man will not lay it over a fence which, quite innocent on the one side, has a twenty-foot drop on the other which might break the neck of both horse and rider; nor will he lay it into a field from which, without some feat of unbelievable daring, there is no way out. But the fox will do both these things and much more besides, and the hot blood of the hounds and the horses and the men and sometimes the women will cause them to follow him over a course which in their sober senses they would never contemplate. And this is the reason, and not the excitement of chasing a small animal, that makes many people prefer fox-hunting to everything else in life, and that makes many more callously impervious to the complaints of people who have never tried it. For, in fact, half the people out hunting seldom see the fox, usually only a handful are there when he is killed, and they do not gloat over his death but often turn their backs, a little sad, and just for the moment a little shamefaced.

117

But, except at this moment, they do not think of the fox, any more than the farmer thinks of the ultimate fate of the bullocks. Once, when I was riding home in the evening with hounds, someone called out to the huntsman:

"Did you kill your fox?"

And he replied:

"No, but we frightened him devilishly."

Now here was a sentence that lends all the colour that is needed to the theory of sadism and blood-lust. But at the time I only thought that the lean, red-faced huntsman had a pictorial turn of phrase. And I am sure that I was right. I am sure that, as captain of a football team, he would have used the same sentence about respected enemies who had triumphed after a well-matched and well-fought game. For the thing about fox-hunting which distinguishes it from such sports as the bullfight, the excitement of which is vicariously felt by spectators, is that everyone shares a little of the risk.

The country in which I hunted was that described by Siegfried Sassoon in *Memoirs of a Fox-hunting Man*, a small country of woods and little fields and little fences, but occasionally a stout post-and-rails and sometimes a brook. At the meet everyone, except those odd, casual figures who do not know fear, is just a little frightened. Often it is very cold, and one's arms ache under the stiff hunting coat, while the horses pull and chafe and occasionally buck. And when one moves off into the woods the older people talk of the hunt of last week and the fences that were jumped, but these are the people who are not going to jump very much, just use their knowledge of the country to keep close to the hounds. The younger ones are usually silent, listening to the hounds and the huntsman, but also feeling what is known as a little windy. And I have been known at this moment to pray that the scent would be bad and the fox a twister, so that one could wait about a while and then trot back home. But soon one begins to splash through the mud in the drives of the wood, and presently, as one becomes a little warmer and the horse settles down, one is

118

ready, when the hounds stream out of the wood across country to gallop out after them. Siegfried Sassoon says in his book that he believes no one enjoys the hunt at the moment of hunting, that it is afterwards in the memory that the pleasure is felt. But surely this is not true. There may always be a little anxiety about what may come next, but there is also a felt happiness when an ugly obstacle has been successfully surmounted. Out hunting no one ever congratulates the rider on his skill or his courage, but there is an implication in the remark: "Your horse jumped the water well." Only a few people in every hunt know well enough what they are doing and have the initiative to lead the way across country; all the rest of the field follow the lead that these have given, but almost every one in his own way exceeds in a good hunt what he would have expected of himself. And so it is true that, when it is all over, and, tired and excessively hungry, one turns for home, and later, when one lies in a bath filled with hot water and mustard to take out the stiffness, or eats eggs and gentleman's relish for tea, the pleasure in the afterthoughts is very great indeed.

The season begins with cub-hunting, and for this one gets up very early, an experience most of the world deny themselves entirely. Since those days I have done it often to milk the cows; and then I have not always wanted to, but have been forced into it, because someone was ill or had left, or someone else was hopelessly incompetent. And then, as I tumbled out of bed and pulled on jeans and a jersey over my pyjamas in answer to a screaming clock, I have cursed and cursed at the men and the cows and the damnable necessity. But always, after I have sleepily pushed my arms into a white milking coat, I have stood outside entranced by the morning light, which is fine and clear but always a little fantastic, and the dew on the grass, and the silence of the sleeping world. And for cub-hunting it was all pleasure, and one felt the illicit excitement of a child who finds himself unexpectedly awake and abroad at the other end of the day. Usually at that time of the year the ground is too hard to do more than walk and trot about and watch the hounds, but occasionally in a wet summer one has a small foretaste of the pleasures to come.

And so I knew much of the greatest happiness of my life during those four curious years. In the summer, as I have said, the riding with Sam Marsh and in the show-ring replaced the hunting. When one looks back to the years of long ago it is the moments of triumph or the moments of failure one chiefly remembers. I had one moment of great triumph in the show-ring and one of humiliation, and both were on the same horse. Some neighbours of ours bred a foal a year from a wonderful old mare, and each year they produced a brilliant youngster out hunting. These horses were usually famous at point-to-points, where year after year they won races. But one year their young horse was also excellent in make and shape. To my pride and surprise, they asked me if I would like to ride him in the Ladies' Hunter class at Richmond Royal Horse Show, one of the great shows of the year. But when I went over to try the horse and rode him in a paddock behind their house, I realised immediately that he had not been schooled for the show-ring and that I myself could not improve him, and also that, although he was good-tempered and kind, his mouth was hard and he was too strong for me. So I rode him back to where his owners stood, and said I thought that in the show-ring, when he was excited by the other horses, I should not be able to hold him. However, everyone pooh-poohed my fears, and the woman who owned him said that she could ride him out hunting with one hand, which I knew to be true because I had seen her do it. So it was decided that I should ride him at Richmond.

In the end it was arranged that Sam Marsh should ride him in the Lightweight Hunter Class and I in the Ladies' Hunters. In the morning at the show Sam took over the horse. First of all he spent a long time making alterations to the fitting of the bit, until he was satisfied. Then he rode him round in circles on the outskirts of the show-ground for half an hour or so. However, when he rode him in the ring, he was turned out in the large bunch of horses the judges discard before they settle down to serious consideration. So that, when I finally mounted him, dressed in a black hunting habit, white stock and top hat, I did so in a bad temper, because I thought I should probably be run away with on a horse that had no chance of a prize. To my amazement the horse under me was unrecognisable. He bent his neck and mouthed at the bit, and, as later we cantered and then galloped round the ring, I found I could hold him, as his owner had said, with one hand. Nevertheless, when the judges called me in first, I thought they were pulling in the horses they were going to turn out as a preliminary to judging the others. Even when this proved untrue, I still thought that they had pulled in the horses in a haphazard way, and that I should go down to the bottom when they made their final placings. It was not until I was handed the red rosette that it occurred to me that I was riding the winner of the Ladies' Hunter Class at Richmond. The reason the judges gave for this reversal of their previous placings was that the horse was too small for the Lightweight Hunter Class, but perfect for a Ladies' Hunter.

However, my pride in this achievement was short-lived. I rode the horse again the following week at the Sussex Show, and Sam Marsh was not there. Turned out by the groom, and having forgotten his lesson, he fulfilled my predictions of the first time I rode him, and it was on him that to my intense humiliation I was forced to turn out of the ring so as to stop.

And this brings me to a matter which is a source of constant amazement to people of my age. In the days of my youth women rode horses that men had schooled for them, and often these horses were returned again and again to be "straightened out." There were a few notable women, but all the great figures in the horse world were men. How is it now, then, that girls of eighteen, often the children of townspeople who know nothing of riding, can take on and beat the world in jumping competitions on horses they have schooled themselves? I have often been asked this question by people who understand the difficulties, and until lately I have always confessed myself equally mystified. A week or two ago I believe I found the answer in my own back-yard.

I have a daughter of twelve, an enthusiastic but moderate horseman. She is too lazy to learn anything, even when I have the energy to try and teach her, and she is also more than a little windy. She has had a succession of ponies, none of which suited her, until lately someone lent her a pony, an unexceptional brown gelding named Humphrey, which she has decided to trust. She rides him saddled and bridled when someone is prepared to help her, on other occasions bareback with a halter on his head.

The other day, as I passed through a small paddock at the back of our house, I was brought to a standstill by astonishment. In the middle of this paddock there was an erection consisting of two five-gallon petrol-drums about five feet away from each other, on the top of each of which there was a two-gallon petrol-can. Between these two uprights, which altogether were about three feet high, there stretched one single thin rail. There were no wings, and the placing of this rickety and inelegant construction was chosen with extraordinary unwisdom in the field where the cows come out from the milking shed, so that the ground on both sides of it was poached and rough. But over the top of the obstacle sailed my daughter on her ordinary pony again and again and again, while a circle of children from the village stood and admired her exploits. I was forced to stand still and consider the matter, and here are the conclusions I drew.

When I was young, children were usually taught to ride by a groom. A groom was normally a countryman who had gone into the stables because at the time there was a vacancy there and not in the garden. He learned to strap and feed a horse and to exercise him, but often he was a stupid man with no particular talent for riding. But by the time he wore polished boots and gaiters and a bowler hat and a stock beneath his jacket, he was regarded as a great authority. In the same way a young horse might be broken by the ham-fisted farmer who bred him, or again by the groom, and neither of these two would necessarily have much time or patience. So, often both horse and rider were spoiled before they ever met each other. In those days, too, it was considered wrong to jump a horse except out hunting, because it was believed that to ask him to jump in cold blood would sicken him.

Nowadays a pony is bought for the children, and for a short time their mother probably takes charge. But soon she is too busy, and the children are left to themselves. Now, children on a pony that frightens them can be pitilessly tetchy, complaining about everything and blaming all their own imperfections on their mount—to the infinite exasperation of their poor mother, who may have spent a small fortune acquiring him. But on a pony which gives them confidence their patience is endless, and their excuses for everything that happens as implausible as are their complaints on the other pony.

"You see, Mummy, I know he was very naughty that time. But I don't think it was his fault. He was just going to do it when that bird flew over. And I don't think he *likes* birds."

Or:

"You see, Mummy, he gave this kind of a jump and I fell off. But I don't think he meant it. I mean I don't think he *knew* I would fall off. I just think he thought it would be funny."

Two or three weeks before I passed through the field where my daughter was showing off to the village children, she had decided to jump her pony. In the first instance one two-gallon petrol-can had been placed on its side at each end of the thin rail, which was thus only about six inches from the ground. The pony had been turned and cantered at this jump during the course of one whole morning. After a while, finding, I suppose, that no one was hurting him, hitting him with a stick, or kicking him with spurs, or jobbing him in the mouth, but also that no one seemed to have anything better to do all day than to keep turning him at this rail, he finally decided to jump it. And then he jumped it again and again. After a while, since it is natural to a horse to jump, with no instructions from the enthusiastic impediment on his back, he was jumping it perfectly, collecting himself at the right moment and taking off in the right place, and actively enjoying it. Then the rail was put up a little higher, and the whole performance repeated, until the feat that I observed was achieved. And if my daughter had had a gift for riding, and if the pony had been an exceptional jumper, then anything in the world might have happened, and, in fact, given these conditions, it does. In Miss Pat Smythe's unexpectedly charming book, *Jump For Joy*, there is a passage in which she talks to her horse while schooling him; and although her words are of a highly professional nature and her patience informed, there is something in her manner of addressing her horse that recalls the notes of my daughter Kate's voice.

" 'When the forelegs leave the ground, they should fold up . . .'

"Hal began to look bored.

" '. . . so that your knees are brought up to your chin . . .

" 'and if you fold them properly, your body will not have to go so high in order to clear the fence . . .

" 'and all this dangling of your legs over a jump is probably no more than over-anxiety . . .

" '. . . so perhaps we could try it again, keeping as calm as possible.'

"And Hal tried it again.

"And again. And again. Experience was what he needed, and what he received."

When I lived in Sussex most of the time that was not spent with horses was occupied by the dogs. I had a large kennel of Alsatians. Buff always held pride of place, although, such was my ambition over small things, there was a short but sad period of coldness between us when I resigned myself to the idea that he was not, as I had believed, of that conformation which wins in the show-ring. He was of an extrovert but extraordinarily willing temperament, and presently, as Field-Trial Champion Buff of Cheyney, he had his area of fame. He was trained to police work in the first place by a professional, but I learned to handle him and did so in all the Field Trials. If his intelligence was not that of a human being, which one is forced against all common sense to believe, he had a miraculous quality of delivering the goods on the day. Once a new exercise was introduced into the Field Trials, and I endeavoured to teach him this myself. Somehow I spoiled him, and reduced him to a state of bewilderment where he would run out in front of me, as the exercise required, but twenty yards away would stop, and, dropping his tail between his legs, turn and regard me questioningly. Then no matter how I tried I could not induce him to go any further, but always had to call him in and attempt it again. So, on the day that I arrived at the ground of the Field Trial, I did so in some shame. He excelled in every other exercise and could only be beaten in this; also it would be obvious to all the professional handlers that he had been spoiled by me. However, when the moment arrived for this particular exercise, he ran out in front of me and stopped twenty yards away as usual, but this time his tail was held high in a question mark; and then he ran on and, for the first time, completed the exercise. This, I suppose, was a coincidence, but it did not feel like one.

The authority on dogs lived on Hayling Island, and, day after day when I was not hunting, I would motor down there with Buff and a bitch named Brunnhilde in the back of the car, and spend the whole day fiddling about with these dogs. And I acquired a dog called Dolf who became a show champion, but was so extraordinarily stupid that he never challenged Buff in my affections. And both these dogs had a satisfactory number of wives, and puppies abounded; but the whole lot lived in the kennels, because I have never cared for dogs in the house.

Then in the last summer of my sojourn in Sussex I fell in with a party of young people who, at the local aerodrome, had taken up flying. They all had a long start of me and most of them had a pilot's certificate before I appeared on the scene. So I tagged along behind as the novice; but I was very happy, because, for the first time since I had left school, I found myself amongst a party of my own contemporaries. This was the smallest licensed aerodrome in England, and, because the flying field was so small, it was difficult to learn to land. There was a club-house where we played darts and drank gin-and-tonics (after we had finished flying), and we all wore white flying overalls and white helmets, which were extremely becoming to the women. There is something that buoys up the ego about all mechanically propelled vehicles, and this is particularly so of an aeroplane.

"Contact," the man said, after one had climbed into the cockpit and adjusted the belt. And:

"Contact," one replied rather grandly, switching on. Then he swung the propeller and the engine roared.

I was not to my chagrin a natural pilot. In the first place, there is some element missing in my nature when it comes to machinery. Weeks later, when I had just landed an aeroplane after a solo flight, someone came up to me and asked:

"Was the oil-pressure like that the whole time you were up?"

And, since I had never looked at the gauge, I had to admit that I had not the slightest idea.

Then, again, I have a sense of direction so defective that, if, slightly lost in a car, I arrive at a T-junction and my instinct tells me to turn left, I invariably turn right, usually with the happiest consequences. The only time I navigated an aeroplane across country it was in the home direction. For a long time we followed a river, but, when near the aerodrome we left it, in a split second I was completely lost. Presently the pilot in the front seat attracted my attention and began to point downwards. I looked immediately at the horizon to see if I was stalling the aeroplane through inattention while trying to find my way, and, reassured on this point, at all the dials on the dashboard, such as the oil-pressure gauge, to try to find out what was wrong. It was only some minutes later that I noticed the hangars and air-stocking of the aerodrome, and realised that he was trying to prevent me from flying right over it. So that, try as I would, I could never become competent in this sphere.

Also, except for the take-off and the landing, which I attacked with the enthusiasm I have for everything I have decided to learn, I have never been able to understand the charm of flying. I never experienced that sense of release and ecstasy alone above the world, which so many people have described. To me it seemed the dullest and the most eventless motion in the world.

So it was a long time before I was ready to fly solo, and in the intervening time events that were to alter many people's lives had taken place. This little flying club and the aerodrome on which it operated were the achievement of a young man of outstanding talents. He was not merely financially the person most involved, and responsible for the organisation, he was one of those figures round whom a small world revolves. During the course of this summer for personal reasons he went away, leaving the group, for whom he had been the star and the centre, feeling as though life had arrested itself in mid-flow. Following this, the whole circle broke up as the holidays came to an end and people returned to their work. So that by September the only people left to play darts in the club-house were a couple of pilots, the girl who was secretary but also an enthusiastic flyer, and myself. We were sad and disconsolate, but we clung together because none of us yet knew what else to do. Outside day after day the weather was grey and rough, the flying difficult, and inside the feeling of flatness and discontent which hits young people so hard in one of these static periods of life could be kept at bay only by a false intimacy and a forced and unreal sense of solidarity. In these circumstances the advent of my first solo flight, which would always have been treated as a matter for a kindly interest, became of great concern to people who felt themselves, temporarily and artificially, to be my close friends.

During the summer there had been two aeroplanes on the airfield for the pupils to fly, an old Avian belonging to the club and a Moth which belonged to a private member, one of our friends. Sometime after the break-up of our party the Moth had been moved away to another commercial flying field. When I sensed that it was now only a question of waiting for a calm day before the pilot-instructor, having seen me complete one tour of the aerodrome, would, after I landed, climb out of the cockpit in front of me, and with an encouraging gesture wave me on my way, I received a telephone call from the owner of the Moth.

"I wondered," he said, "if you are thinking of flying solo. Because before you do, I think you ought to know that the Moth has been put on a stand at Heston as a demonstration of the degree of unairworthiness an aeroplane can get to without actually breaking up in the air."

Now this was a statement exactly as frightening to me as it would be to anyone else who has an irrational fear of the air, that is to say a fear not felt in motor-cars or trains, and uninfluenced by comparative statistics of accidents. I have said that I was not naturally a pilot, and, although I no longer felt every time I climbed into an aeroplane that just because I was in it something untoward would occur, neither had I ever acquired the superb confidence given to those more accomplished in the air. In the matter of courage I am about as brave as is taken for granted, although, to show off, I occasionally in those days forced myself a bit. But the courage of people who seek out and laugh at danger, which one reads of in books about the war, is as far off from me and as uncomprehended as the ability to write music.

I took a day off from the aerodrome to consider what I had been told. In the first place it was possibly untrue, or it might be highly exaggerated. The little circle of friends at the aerodrome had not been broken up without hurt, or without emotions which might grossly colour statements of fact. On the other hand it might be true. The ground-staff at the aerodrome, headless now for some time, depressed and disorganised, might be incapable of maintaining an aeroplane at the necessary pitch of mechanical perfection. I knew that there was a system of inspection and licensing carried out by the Ministry, but I did not know how often or how recently this had taken place. I did not feel that what I had been told could be ignored. The risk seemed to be not that the aeroplane in which I flew solo would break up in the air, but that something less catastrophic might happen which would entail a forced landing. And I was very nearly certain that, should this happen, I was incapable of the necessary skill.

The method of landing an aeroplane in those days (everything seems to be quite different now) was as follows. At a certain point, above and off the aerodrome, one switched off the engine. From then on it was a matter of judgment to circle slowly round and in against the wind, until, when one hovered over the air-field, one had lost sufficient height to stall and plop down on to it. If one undershot it was possible to use a little engine to make up the distance, if one overshot the only thing one could do was to open the throttle and fly round again to repeat the approach. There was, in fact, a method of losing height called side-slipping, which, by a combination of joystick and one brake-pedal, caused the aeroplane to lose height quickly by a kind of skid through the air. But, for some reason that I never understood, one did not practise this before flying solo, but only afterwards if one went on to try for higher grades of skill. I had seen it done often enough, and I believed it to be quite easy to manage, but I had never tried it. The aerodrome itself was quite difficult to land on because it was so very small and surrounded on three sides by a dyke and on the fourth by the hangers. Later, when I once landed an aeroplane at Heston, it seemed to me one had the whole world before one. Nevertheless, I could hardly have missed the airfield, because for weeks I had circled round over it, switching off at more or less the same place. I felt absolutely unconvinced, however, that if the engine petered out in the air so that one had to estimate distance in a split-second of panic on to a neighbouring field, without help if one undershot or the ability to fly on if one overshot, I should be able to do it. This, I think, was because I was such an untalented pilot; I ought by now to have been capable of it.

Consequently I took the message from my friend quite seriously. I can see now that this may have been unnecessarily cowardly or unusually self-important. The mathematical chances might have been adequately reassuring, since I had been flying the aeroplane dual for weeks without anything happening. In any case I have never lost a distrust of the air that to this day causes me a small feeling of relief when the wheels of an aeropnlae touch down smoothly onto the ground, and at that time I had a quite rational fear of my own capacity. In peacetime one is trained to take care, not to encounter unnecessary risk. I therefore considered matters of life and death.

There were three things I could do. The first was to forget the message and go ahead with the solo flight. The second was to refuse to go solo on the grounds of the message. The third to refuse to go solo, giving no reason for this unexpected resolve. The decision I made may have been due to the fact that my moral cowardice was greater than my physical, but this was not how it appeared to me. For the first time I looked back over my twenty-four years, and thought that they had been unexpectedly pointless. I had never been unhappy—indeed I thought then that some strong feeling might have added depth and consequence— but equally it seemed to me that nothing in my life had had any greater significance than that of passing the time. I was not concerned with the meaning of the universe; my thoughts were only of myself. They were not influenced by a religious upbringing, by any philosophy, or much by the thoughts of other men, because, as I hope I have shown, I had grown up quite free of these things. I had no inner life of the spirit, although I have always enjoyed the pleasures of thought. Most noticeable to me was the absence of love: at this time, and for several years to come, I believed myself in any sustained, passionate or self-immolating way, incapable of that emotion. I thought that, if I refused to go solo, I should, by embarrassing and disappointing the already discouraged little group of people on the aerodrome, be sacrificing to life the only kind of grace by which it appeared to be dignified. I wondered then, as I often have since, why so much importance is attached to the length of the short span of our time in this world. And if I have dwelt on this incident for longer than it deserves, it is because for some years these thoughts were constantly to return to me.

The following day was quite calm, though still grey and

130

depressing. After I had completed one tour of the aerodrome, and, landing on the field, taxied round to take off again, the pilot climbed out of the cockpit in front of me and swept me a bow. I gave the engine full throttle, and, pulling the joystick back slowly, accomplished the take-off successfully. Once in the air, I am certain that I was not in the least frightened, but, in a rational and detached mood, I noticed that the aeroplane was behaving in a manner that seemed to me highly unusual. Presently I happened to glance at the hand which held the joystick, and I saw that it was trembling so violently that the aeroplane was waggling about in the air. Once I understood what was happening, I was able to control it, and I completed the circuit and flopped down on the airfield with plenty of room to spare. Then I walked into the club-house for drinks and congratulations.

But this was the end. I flew solo several times more and for longer, but I never completed the three hours necessary before applying to be tested for a pilot's certificate. I had tasted during that summer the pleasures of youth and companionship, and I felt cold and empty and deserted. I knew that I could not settle down to face another long winter with no one but the horses and the dogs to warm the cockles of the heart. Nor, I knew quite well, had I any real comfort to give, or actual obligation to the dejected little group on the aerodrome. It seemed to me that the push I had been waiting for had arrived at the exact moment I had expected it. So one day I packed my bags and left the house in Sussex, and, although I did not do this entirely without regrets or even without tears, I never went back.

9

DURING the early nineteen-thirties I lived in London, at first in the house of a friend. In those days it was unusual for women who belonged to families rich enough to keep them to do any work at all. There was no taboo against it, and women with some talent, say for dressmaking, or interior decoration, for acting or for writing, often found employment; but women were neither qualified for routine jobs nor expected to do them. Nor was the task of running a house very arduous. Households were very much smaller and simpler than they had been before the 1914 war, and if they were adequately staffed, an interview with the cook in the morning was probably the most required of the mistress of the house. She might, however, be put to some trouble in ensuring that her house was adequately staffed, because, in spite of unemployment, domestic service was already looked on with much disfavour. More time than was regarded as reasonable or enjoyable might have to be spent in employment agencies, but, when this matter was satisfactorily settled, the task of women of the upper classes was to fill whole lives of leisure.

They were curiously deprived of natural occupation. The days of letter-writing were past. A telephone beside the bed, in almost continuous use between nine-thirty and eleven o'clock every morning, took care of the need for communication. In the same way journeys were now so simple and so quickly made that elaborate plans, family upheavals, considered packings, were also a thing of the past. Children were taken care of by nannies and nursery-maids. Excessive family preoccupation was a bourgeois trait, and it took an original mind to conceive that time outside the limited and conventional hours prescribed for the purpose might be spent with the children. Many years later a young man whose adult behaviour was a source of unhappiness to his parents said to me;

"My parents have no right to complain of me. Until I was old enough to be amusing I practically never saw them."

"But that's not true," I protested in amazement and distress. "Your mother adored you."

"She may have," he replied, "but I never saw her except at the week-end, and then with never less than about eighteen people. The rest of my life was spent with the servants."

I think he exaggerated. I think his mother kept him with her as much as her life allowed. I know that she often took him with her to other people's houses. But I think that, when he looked back in memory to his childhood, he might well have believed it to be as he described it to me. Nor would it be true to suggest that all children were as neglected as this one. It is true, however, that their welfare did not make employment for their mothers.

Single women, then, and young married women filled their lives with a round of social engagements. When I arrived in London at the age of twenty-five, I found that, unless I was going to live a very solitary life, it was necessary to dine out nearly every evening, lunch out every day, and go to the country most week-ends. This was merely a question of knowing enough people, because entertaining, both in London and in country houses, large and small, was constant. A great deal of it was simpler than in the preceding paragraphs I may have made it sound. One played golf during the day with another woman, or lunched alone with a friend. All the houses one visited at the week-end were not large or grand, although I think they all had resident servants. It was seldom that I packed or unpacked for myself. A great many clothes were necessary. One nearly always changed for dinner, even in country houses, where one wore either what today would be termed "full evening dress," or what was then, I think, still called a "teagown," and resembled the housecoat of today except that it was of more elaborate cut and material. Appropriate clothes could not be bought ready-made as they are today, but were chosen from models and made individually. One needed clothes for London and clothes for the country, since these were not almost interchangeable as they are now—a tweed coat and skirt, for instance, for the country and a black one for London. During the whole of the time I spent in London I never had enough clothes, or ones that seemed to me suitable for any particular occasion, and, because I was young and extremely conventional, this added very much to a social shyness which was caused by the fact that I was moving in a world in which I had not been born and where I did not know many people. I hardly ever knew everyone in a room, or, at a week-end party, everyone in the house, and since the basis of most conversation is gossip, this was a constant difficulty.

After I had been about a year back in London, my father, who was restless and unhappy, decided to give up his flat and to take a house which I could share with him. We found a very charming small house in Wilton Place, and, before we moved in, we spent a great deal of money on it. It was ideal for two people because it had, on separate floors, two sets of three rooms, a bedroom, sitting-room and bathroom. My father viewed our life there in advance in a pictorial way. He saw that we would live there separate lives of an independent dignity, but that we would come together several times a week to give little dinner or luncheon parties. He fussed extremely about my arrangements for the decoration and furnishing of the house, because, having no taste, he could not judge them. I remember that one of the things I bought was a set of earthenware vegetable-dishes about which he was very doubtful, because he could not remember having seen this type of thing before. When at our first luncheon party these were admired, he said to me afterwards:

"Don't tell everyone where you got them. We will keep them for ourselves."

We achieved a first-class cook, a butler, a housemaid, and a between-maid, and, as far as money could buy it, we had the setting for the life he visualised. Never for a second, however, did it fulfil his dreams. In the picture of our parties that he had seen in his mind there had always been one or two eligible young men, sitting next to me and paying me courteous attention. He was quite modest in his requirements. They need not be the sons of peers, nor even very rich. If they had been intelligent, well set up in some job, and morally of average character this would have satisfied him. Unfortunately in reality they did not appear at our parties. I had made many friends in London by this time, but they were either friends of my father's, in the main young married couples and their attendants of both sexes, or people from other worlds of whom he could not approve, a young artist or two, some quite dim young married couples, and, his particular *bête noire,* a clever, practically starving and I must admit, unusually dirty female novelist. When he did not distrust the intentions of the men I knew, he feared them—they were so eminently ineligible. He regarded my life as wilfully mis-conducted. From the moment I left Sussex, his only hope for me was to see me re-married, and the pressure towards this end was now redoubled and reinforced by the views of all his friends. It seems never to have occurred to anyone that I might possibly have liked to get married myself, or that the humiliation caused me by the constant plotting and spying might make this desired objective more difficult to achieve. Not that it would have made any great difference to our relationship if these thoughts had occurred to him. He was an entirely instinctive character, and one was either pleasant and successful, a source of pride, or else one was a constant irritation.

We quarrelled therefore incessantly, and within six months we had got rid of the house and each of us had separately taken a flat. After this our relationship improved, but, during the time we lived together, I think for the only time in his life, he actively disliked me. He was a man of intense generosity, but, in relation only to his family, he liked to have value for money. During the time that I lived with him, he began to resent the money I cost him. It was for this reason more than any other that he presently announced that I must look for a job. I do not think that he believed I would succeed in finding one that he would regard as

135

satisfactory; I think his intention was simply to be beastly, and to give himself a further source of grievance against me. He would never have countenanced a job that took me out of London, or away from the world in which husbands are found.

Life at this time was naturally exceedingly irksome to me. I resented bitterly my dependence upon him, and my humiliation was the more complete because I was aware that this was an inescapable fact. It was a surprise and a pleasure therefore to both of us when, almost by accident, I landed a job in London in which I was paid the, for that time, quite large sum of £5 a week. There was no question of my being able to live the kind of life that I was leading on this wage, but it was a contribution, and my father, who in fact loved me, was aware that I worked hard in my job and he became more sympathetic towards me.

One night, sitting next to a man who was the head of a very big business which had offices and a showroom in London, I had suggested that he might find me a job.

"The trouble with you girls," he replied, "is that you can none of you do shorthand or typing."

On the strength of the shorthand I had learned at school and of the typing that had been done in the main by my father's secretary for Sir Patrick Hastings, I told him that this was quite untrue and that I was capable of both. However, something in the way he received this remark suggested that he might take it seriously, and for a few weeks I went to a shorthand school in the mornings in an attempt to make good my boast. In consequence, by the time I was installed as personal secretary (one of two) to the head of one of the biggest manufacturing firms in England, although my typing was a matter for ribaldry to every other secretary in the building, I was able to bluff my way through. I could not have done this if I had attempted to take down dictation in the form it was given, for I could not approach the necessary speed. From the first day I simply took down the sense of the matter, and wrote the letters in my own words. These were sufficiently more graceful than those that had been hurriedly dictated, and so gave pleasure, and I may have owed the fact that I held down this job partly to the inadequacy of my shorthand, which forced me to give time and thought to these letters. The typing was another matter. No letter was ever signed in this office which had a single mistake in it, and, owing to the fact that my employer dealt with his correspondence spasmodically, on days when he elected to answer it there was an enormous amount of work to be got through. I had never learned to type by what is called the touch system, and nothing except the hardest work and concentration enabled me on these days to hammer my way through the work allotted to me. For the first three months of my employment I felt physically ill. I was unable to sleep at night, and at home I used constantly to burst into tears on the slightest or no provocation. I was astonished at the hardness of the life of office workers, although the capacity to endure this, unnatural and unhealthy as it is, seems to be largely a matter of training, because after about three months I got used to it.

From the first I was impressed and touched, as people of my class are apt to be, by the kindness and sympathy of the rest of the staff. I could hardly have survived the first months of my inexperience without their help, which was freely offered in spite of the obvious facts that I owed my position to nepotism, and that, because the only thing I had to contribute to this office was a manner and personality unusual in the circumstances, I was immediately given nearly all the plums of secretarial work. It was the first time I had come into close contact with working-class girls, and I was shocked by their conditions and touched by their lives. Typists were very badly paid in those days and extremely hard-worked. Two other women in the whole business earned as much as I did, and one of them, like myself, owed it to an upper-class personality. Other secretaries earned £3 or £3–10–0 a week, and the large pool of ordinary typists were paid twenty-five shillings. Most of them subsisted on buns and coffee or tea, and their clothes were few and poor. They were often treated, in my view, with insufficient courtesy, but this applied also to more senior members of the staff. In these days of full employment it is inconceivable that offices could be run on the lines and in the atmosphere of that time.

Nowadays, when people think of the unemployment of the twenties and thirties they think of grey-faced, sullen men standing on the streets of Wigan and Jarrow, of under-nourished, bow-legged children, of the Means Test, and the terrible resignation. What everyone seems to have forgotten is that when you have declining productivity, it affects every class and every person. In those days in the middle as well as the lower classes a job successfully landed for one's son was almost as much a matter for rejoicing as a husband for one's daughter, and no one, even those successfully placed, ever felt quite secure. Nowadays one hears so much talk of the lack of incentive in England. Everyone seems to have forgotten what a terrible disincentive it was not to have a job at all.

This insecurity bred corruption in the relations of society. When any job that falls vacant can be filled a dozen times the next morning, the power of employers is too great. It was no uncommon thing for the head of a business to send for an executive who, in his opinion, had made some trifling mistake, and, in front of two or three people, address him in terms and with a manner devastating to his self-respect. And the job of an intelligent, educated and sensitive man with a wife and child was to stand there in silence, afterwards to be only gradually revived by the half-expressed sympathy and encouragement of his fellow-employees.

The power of the unions to strike was used again and again, but the power of the unions to protect their members from gross abuse in the performance of their jobs was nullified by the fear of unemployment. Typists in offices, living on a pittance, could be kept at work until ten o'clock at night at the whim of the great man. For this they got no overtime; sometimes they did not even get thanked.

It was easy, coming in fresh from outside, to feel indignation on their behalf, and once when I was given an opportunity to express my views to those in power, I did so with unconcealed relish.

I take no credit for this because I was by now in a strong position in the firm, and in any case I had nothing important to lose.

These offices were in a new building, and, since they were often visited by important customers, minor government officials and so on, a great deal of money and trouble had been spent to give them an elegant appearance. Every visitor to the offices of the senior staff had, however, to pass through a square open space where sat at work the pool of typists, probably twenty girls. Now in those days, as George Orwell remarked, there was an impassable barrier between the upper and lower classes because the upper classes thought the lower classes smelled. On a hot summer's day this group of girls drew the attention of everyone who walked by to the fact that this was no mere whimsey of the upper classes. One day I was called into the office of my employer and asked to undertake a task of special difficulty and delicacy. I then had it haltingly explained to me that it was a source of embarrassment and discomfort to the heads of this business that as they passed, often with a distinguished visitor, through the typists' pool their nostrils should be assaulted in this way. I was asked if I would therefore make an enquiry into the matter to find out how these girls could be educated to a more mannerly and sympathetic bodily condition.

I think I immediately appreciated the full stupidity of this suggestion. In any case, I remember settling down delightedly and in a spirit of considerable impertinence to my reply.

"Are you serious?" I asked. "Because if so I think I can tell you immediately and without any research what might be done."

I then explained that not to smell is an expensive thing. One needs to own more than one dress which, too thin in the winter, is too thick in the summer, and also many sets of underclothes, so that these can be frequently changed. Hot water and plenty of soap are also essential and not easily obtained in working-class houses. Then again I explained, warming in the silence of the room to my task, where twenty girls sit together it is better to have a few windows and not rely for light and air entirely on electric lamps and fans.

139

"I understand," I finally remarked, "that each of these girls earns twenty-five shillings a week. I think if you were to double this immediately, it would be possible for me to explain to them how you wanted some of the increase spent."

All this was as ill-received as I had expected it to be, and I sat through a lecture on the theme: the difference between profit and loss is overheads. I did not know then that this was the same argument that had been used in one form or another for keeping children of five at work in factories, or miners at work in pits that were unsafe, but I did realise that, in a firm with the turnover of this one and in relation to a sum of money of the size under discussion, it was an argument that smelled at least as badly as the girls, and I made no pretence of not noticing this. Relations between myself and my employer were cool for a few days, but this was the only outcome of his enquiry.

Personally I was always very well treated. I still went out almost every night in London and away to the country for many week-ends, and since in some ways it suited my employer that I should do so, ordinary office hours were not enforced. I was, nevertheless, almost always short of sleep, and because all our offices had glass walls, I became adept at falling asleep in positions that appeared entirely business-like. In spite of this, I also worked extremely hard at times when it was necessary. I had a strong ambition at first to rise in this firm, because I was enchanted by the notion of achieving complete independence. I learned quite soon that there was little prospect of that, however. This was not because it was so completely out of the question that some woman might have risen to a job on the administrative staff—although none, I think, ever did—but because I had neither the talents nor the training for any position higher than the one I occupied. I was interested in the work I did, however, and I stayed quite happily in this job for about eighteen months until I married for the second time.

10

THE younger generation of the nineteen-fifties seem to me in general to have incomparably more interesting and fuller lives than young men and women have ever known before, in spite of their never having known the wealth and leisure which in retrospect seem so much a matter for regret. The only thing that I remember from my youth which I feel my daughter reasonably might envy was the scale of the country houses and of the entertaining which went on there.

The English have a talent for country-house life which has bloomed through the centuries as unaffectedly as the great cabbage-roses they grow in their gardens. Once, in the eighteenth and early nineteenth centuries, this talent was nurtured in an environment so warmly agreeable that it became the inspiration for one of the golden ages of art. During this short period, when economic power was still concentrated in the landed interest, it was used to build great houses, to plan stately gardens, to mould and form the landscape into a proper setting for the pillared and porticoed grace that rose amongst it, to commission paintings, tapestry, carpets, furniture, china, glass, to span little streams with elegant stone bridges, to decorate England with domed lodges and arched gateways, to experiment fancifully with temples, terraces, follies.

Nowadays, when on a summer's day I go with my children to pay my half-crown and visit one of the relics of this ennobling age, and, as likely as not, we drive out of the sun on to the narrow road beneath the magnificent trees which for the millionth time perform their function of stilling the small movements of the mind before the eye shall light on the splendour that lies ahead, I am invaded by sadness. It is not that I have so great an inclination to turn the clock back—less, in fact, than many of my contemporaries—nor yet that I have so much love for the ghosts of the people who once lived here, or sorrow for their descendants deprived of the most glorious part of their inheritance. I was born with so little of the quality of homage that I cannot bewail the loss to one small group of people of what so few could share. No, it is for the still, cold, sterile emptiness of the great house itself that my heart is touched to regret.

These unforgettable monuments to the higher nature of man— as incomprehensible in our progressive age as the stones of the cathedrals which rise worshipfully into the sky—were built to house a warm and glowing life, a life no more artificial and seemingly no less splendid than their own moulded ceilings and carved and polished doorways, a life which, if it was surrounded by a poverty and squalor which we are no longer prepared to contemplate, was at least capable of this vigorous act of creation. For, as Lord David Cecil has pointed out, these houses were not palaces, and the lives pursued beneath their roofs were not unreal. This was simply the most perfect phase of the English talent for drawing-rooms, for libraries, for lofty, chintz-covered bedrooms, for gardens, for horses and dogs, for leisure, for a guiltless and gracious feeling for space and privacy, for good living and love of the land.

So now, as one wanders behind a chattering guide through the lovely rooms, and gazes at the perfection of the useless furniture, as one buys the picture-postcards and notes the ice-cream booths, I for one am so oppressed by the emptiness of the crowded house, by the loss of function of the neglected home, that I think I would gladly relinquish my right to view such splendours if this would fire once more the wood beneath the marble chimney-pieces, light the great chandeliers, and people the rooms with moving figures dressed in rich materials, with men and women born to believe in their right to be there.

It is then that I catch myself in one of the most common of human weaknesses; for I find that I am identifying myself not with the crowd amongst whom I have paid my half-crown, but with the house and the families that once inhabited it. And I wonder, is this as natural as the instinct by which I identify myself with the heroine of a play, or is it a cheap nostalgia which, obliterating the humdrum daily life, reaches back to the romantic moments of a half-forgotten youth? I notice that when I am with people younger than myself they seem not to feel as I do, to be unaware of the ghostlike presence of unfulfilment, like that of parted lovers, but to move through the house with the absorbed detachment that I might feel in a mediaeval castle or a Roman villa deserted by history long ago.

In the 1920s and 30s the English talent for country-house life in the grand manner, already almost a thing of the past, was in its final phase. After the 1914 war the wealth was never again so great, the servants were not so plentiful, many of the great houses were already closed. But the virtues of the British upper classes could be seen at their best in those houses which were still lived in. They had a kind of simplicity in the country which I had not met in the more frivolous world I had known in London, a natural rootedness in their surroundings which I doubt if any other nation has so beautifully produced. The women had a graceful gift for keeping extremely busy all day long doing almost nothing, and this was extremely attractive to me, because, born in less gentle and less assured surroundings, I have a demon of nervous energy which needs to be driven harder. They loved their gardens and would spend hours talking to the gardener, weeding the rock-garden or planning the new border. The men went shooting in rough old clothes, while the women visited some favourite tenant to bring home a ham specially smoked for the dining-room, or discussed with a secretary the arrangements for the village fête. It was no uncommon thing to stand talking to an outside servant, and, turning with a smile of complicity for his unsophisticated enthusiasm, to see the same honest emotion reflected on one's host's face.

Usually there would be a large colony of dogs—gun-dogs outside in the stables, but inside the dogs that were loved for no utilitarian reason, but because they were fat, or excessively stupid, or for the trouble they gave the butler when he came to

143

put them out in the evenings. I have known a whole house-party queue up night after night to watch the performance of this last dog. The butler, conscious of a loss of face, played his part in the evening's entertainment, with a struggle for dignity but without resentment. And I know now, from running a farm, that this was remarkable. If on a farm one once allows a man to lose face, he will leave as soon as he can think of an excuse unconnected with the incident, and it is the constant preoccupation of a wise employer to prevent this happening. But these people silently and decorously teased this manservant again and again, and he took it all in good part. He had a consciousness of privilege now lost, but also he was aware of love.

The house that I knew best was not of the great period, nor on the largest scale. It was a grandchild of the great Whig houses, built for a younger son at a time when the natural philistinism of the English had outlived the short moment of a power so supreme as to be an inspiration for artists, architects, and gardeners. It was, in fact, an ugly house, but even in its ugliness it was so simple and uninhibited, so informed with the serenity and the feeling for space and leisure of its former owners, that it exercised a sturdy charm. It had not sixty bedrooms, but it could and did house eighteen or twenty guests at a week-end, and it could reasonably be said to represent all that was best and most typical of English hospitality at that time. The days of the greatest splendour were over, but, and this had a particular delight for guests from humbler spheres, the formality too had gone.

Luxury itself is very beguiling when it is composed of sensitive things. In ordinary houses beds do not seem to have such thick, ensnaring softness, nor is the linen so fine. Nowadays, too, one does not go to sleep as one did then, for all but about three months in the year, in the light of the flickering flames of a fire. This is an almost forgotten pleasure, but very seductive. The young are susceptible to the trappings of wealth and I felt in this house a consciously sensuous pleasure.

I went there with my father and I loved it. When I think about it now I am filled with the same impersonal sadness. I do not wish myself there again. I have grown too far away from the person I was in my youth. But I grieve that, although the house still stands, the household that lived in it is a thing of the past.

But the graces of country-house society in England were almost entirely private ones, and hardly extended beyond the confines of the garden. Around lay the farms, impoverished and under-capitalised. Cottages and buildings fell into disrepair for the unquestioned reason that it was not a paying proposition to maintain them. It was one of the ugliest aspects of England between the wars, this ruthless neglect of the countryside by a country-loving nation. By the time I travelled round England looking for a farm at the beginning of the second world war, the desolation was complete. There were whole villages in which there was not a single plough, not a single water-tap, and no drains. On the farms the buildings were falling down, the thatch caved in and smelling of must, the bricks and rubble overgrown with nettles. There were no fences, no roads and no water. Often the stock of several hundred acres would be a few milking cows, lying in short standings, continually slapping their tails against the flies, and a few hens scratching about in the rickyard. The derelict appearance of the farmyards was often increased by the hulks of disused American cars. The only implement the farmers ever seemed to own was a hay-sweep, and this they drove with someone's cast-off car because they could not afford a tractor. The atmosphere of defeat and depression was so pervasive that often one left a farm without looking further than the house and buildings, so strong was the conviction that one could not start out on a new adventure in this rotting smell of failure. The farms that were on the market at that time were not as a rule broken recently off from some large estate, but often belonged to owner-occupiers, sometimes to men who twenty years before had turned hopefully to the land in the aftermath of the first war. Nevertheless, it is true to say that today, after twenty years of regeneration, many of the farms that still have cottages without water or drains, buildings that defeat the principles of modern agricultural science, are on the estates of the large landowners, where no single fortune has been able to repair the ravages of the nineteen twenties and thirties.

When agriculture was referred to in the houses where I stayed, it was usually with the gentle irony accorded the servants and the dogs.

"My wife has decided to go in for pig-farming, so one can count on a slump in pigs."

This irony covered all deficiencies, and they were many. For, if this was an intelligent world, it was almost entirely philistine, assured but uncultivated, honourable but uncreative. It lived almost entirely on the fat of the past, a decoration but not a contribution to the life of the time.

No longer the inspiration for art, it no longer understood or cared for such things. In those days there was still enough money to have formed small collections of paintings, to have bought the pictures which now go for ten to twenty times the price to America. But the artists of the time drew no impulse from, were not nourished in this quiet, composed scene, as they had been a century or so before, and the pictures that they painted had no place in the country houses of England. So alien were they, in fact, that even the instinct of the rich for investment slept in peace. Talent and appreciation were not unknown among the aristocracy of England, but they were no more conspicuous here than anywhere else in the world, and, where taste existed, it no longer found employment in the forefront of a movement, but was as quietly and unassumingly behind the times as the taste of the general public. It would have been possible to find a little Renoir treasured somewhere in one of these houses, or a Sickert, or a John, but one might have searched for many a day before one found a Picasso or a Braque. In the same way the taste for literature was usually intelligent, but it was not discriminating, and music was all too often represented only by a gramophone which, mechanically changing the records, played as a background to conversation, and occasionally through a defect in the changing-device played the same tune again and again, unheard through the spirited conversation—a form, it now seems, of self-torture much enjoyed in those days.

All that was left of power now was politics, and this was not merely a matter of burning interest, it was a matter of personal concern. Yet they were all political innocents.

This is not surprising. I have met many politicians in my life of different political colours, and the one figure I find it impossible to believe in is the Bismarckian manipulator, the statesman capable of giving history the smallest foresighted push. It often happens that the views or actions of politicians are a matter for wonder to the general public.

"Ah!" one thinks then. "They know, of course, something that we don't know."

And this indeed is the trouble. Statesmen are seldom peculiarly stupid, nor do they so quickly grow out of touch with the spirit of the times as is sometimes thought; but they have access to information, and unaware that, as often happens, this is entirely misleading, they place confidence in it. The broad uninformed view of the public can sometimes be more sensitive to reality. In the early spring of 1940 I lunched at the house of a Minister of the Crown. Asked his opinion of the course of the phoney war, he replied:

"I agree with Halifax. What we needed was time, and what they have given us is time. I believe that Hitler has reached an impasse, and it is difficult for him to know what move to make."

I have no idea whether Lord Halifax himself ever made the remark attributed to him, I only know what was said at luncheon that day. But I find no difficulty in believing that he did say it, and I quote it as a convenient but not as an isolated example of the foreknowledge of politicians. Whether they are talking of bus-strikes or of major wars, it is my experience that politicians, with an outspokenness that to a member of the public never ceases to be surprising, commit themselves to unexpected views that are often proved wrong within a week. I have come to the conclusion that the only thing that makes it possible for them to continue in their positions unabashed is that by the time events

147

have given them the lie, new matters engage their minds, new views are being formulated. I speak here without facetiousness. History confirms my view. In the great days of power it may have been possible for statesmen to make accurate predictions because they could back them with overwhelming force. During the whole course of my lifetime they have been led like children from one event to another. What makes the statesmen of the nineteen thirties seem so exceptionally innocent is, in the first place, the years that lay in front of them, but, in the second, the fact that they still believed implicitly in the prerogative, the duty of their class to run the country.

They were immune to outside opinion. It did not make them angry; they thought it tiresome or ridiculous. In the early nineteen thirties an upper-class member of the Tory party believed Stafford Cripps a "gift," and Hitler "finished." They were more uncertain about Mussolini. They thought him a highly ridiculous figure, but he had made the trains run to time, and while some admired him, others realised uneasily that he might be too much of a thug safely to hold such power.

Once in a country house I heard the question of mass unemployment discussed in the presence of two Cabinet Ministers.

"Why don't you set them to work building roads?" asked a young man of unusually radical opinions.

"Where do we get the money?" one of the two great men asked.

"Well," the young man replied, "you make it, as you will have to in the war that will presently come upon you."

This remark was both tiresome and nearly unanswerable. The two men did not notice that it was unanswerable, but they did notice that it was tiresome. They brushed it aside with the manner of nannies at a tea-party where someone else's child, some infant immune to reproof, shows evidence of a spoilt and silly nature. And so would they have brushed aside any remark not emanating from a political philosophy conceived beneath this or a similar roof.

This psychological or emotional immunity to outside views,

148

a common weakness of mankind, causes naturally tender-hearted people to behave at times in a singularly heartless way. In the slump of 1927 and again in 1931, with two million men unemployed, the owners of country houses, acting entirely from what they understood to be their patriotic duty, cut down the numbers of their house-servants. In the house which I knew well the guests, equally patriotic, reacted to the situation by coming down for breakfast. This meant that breakfast had to be kept hot in the dining room until after eleven o'clock, while the bedrooms were not freed earlier than usual. Aware of the despair of the remaining servants, our host finally ordered his guests to breakfast in bed.

In 1931 I took, for the only time in my life, an active part in a general election. This election was fought, after a short period of Labour rule, to preserve the Gold Standard. My part in this affair was the humble one of addressing envelopes and canvassing. This was a strongly held Conservative seat, but included certain parts of an industrial town that were known to be Labour. After a few days it transpired that some streets in this town had been excluded from the canvass, because the local Conservative workers believed their inhabitants to be so red as to be dangerous. No one was prepared to face the rough rudeness that might be expected there. In our house-party this was regarded as a little absurd, and one of the women volunteered for the task.

"And you," she said to me, "can come with me."

For one long day we travelled up and down the narrow, ugly streets of slum houses, calling at each and talking to the occupants. During the whole day we seldom saw a man, although where they were I do not know, because they were probably not at work. At each of the doors we were met by the vile smell of boiling clothes, a characteristic of working-class houses, and by an apathetic drab of a woman. There were two stock replies to our question. The more common was:

"None of it matters to us. It's all the same for us whoever gets in."

The other:

149

"Oh! we shall vote for the Conservatives. They are the people with the money. They must know best how to look after it."

When we reported at night the bathetic results of our brave adventure, no single person was touched by any emotion other than amusement at the tameness of our encounters, or impatience with the working class that could not be made to use their votes to save the country. Nor had I been during the day. In a society where the differences between rich and poor are very great, and where the inevitability of this difference is taken for granted, the separation between the classes is so wide that most people cannot make the necessary effort of imagination to feel the lives of the other half as real.

11

AFTER I left the house I shared with my father I found by an extraordinarily lucky chance, for it was not easy, a very attractive small flat. This was a converted L-shaped London drawing-room that had been divided at the junction of the L into a sitting-room and bedroom, with a kitchen and bathroom down a small flight of steps. I had a full-time maid who had very little to do, and I had a small car. On the night that I moved into this flat I only wondered desperately how long I should live there, and in what circumstances I should move out.

Basically I was exceedingly discontented. There was a kind of negativeness about my life which, I believe, is the lot of nearly every normal young woman before marriage. Superficially it was full and entertaining, but at moments when I was alone—in August, for instance, when I was left at work in London while all my friends had gone to the country—I felt an impassioned discontent which was more unhappy than any experience I have suffered since. It was then I used to wonder, as I had in the aeroplane days, about the pointlessness of life. So strong is the urge of women towards a home of their own, a man and children, that no other experience is felt in depth.

It was on my twenty-eighth birthday that I was given a present by a young man I had known for only a week or two—a complete recording of the opera *La Traviata,* consisting of about fifteen records in a red buckram case. This seemed an unexpected setback. My experience of opera had stopped short at the disappointment in Brussels when we had been taken to hear *The Marriage of Figaro,* but I had the idea that my life might depend on my reception of this present. In young ladies the desire to please is a major biological force, but could it, I wondered, turn me into a lover of opera? I approached the matter methodically.

Somehow I had acquired the knowledge that where works of art are concerned familiarity may help appreciation. In my flat there was a gramophone with a record-changing mechanism that could play eight records consecutively. From the time that I received this present, while I dressed in the mornings and again in the evenings, during any meal that I had at home, and at all other times that I was alone in the flat, the music of *La Traviata* filled the small rooms. But I did not listen to it. For a child of the twenties, accustomed to background music, this presented no problem, and I continued to think my thoughts or read my book quite undisturbed by the tremendous flow of sound. It took rather more than a week. At the end of that time, as I applied the eyeblack to my eyelashes one evening, I found that I was humming abstractedly to the accompaniment of the gramophone. This was the first time that I consciously heard the drinking song in the first act of *La Traviata*, but, elated by the success of my method, I found some minutes later that I could also hear, if not yet hum, the love song. This was my introduction to music. I cannot say that I have never looked back, because, as a matter of fact, I stick at the late Beethoven quartets, the whole of Wagner, and at much modern music. But twenty years later, during which time the desire to please has grown much enfeebled and has lost its miraculous powers, I find it possible to live in a house where everyone's idea of a present to another member of the family is a long-playing gramophone record, I accompany my husband as often as two or three times a week to Covent Garden in the opera season, while *The Marriage of Figaro* is only less delightful to me than *La Traviata*. My children, born as unmusical as I am, but subjected to the strains of the gramophone from birth, could truthfully be described as ardent lovers of music.

My father welcomed Jack into the family in characteristic style. He had conceived the idea that it was barbaric to expect people to like other people merely because they were related by marriage. So as to convey to Jack that nothing of this sort would be required, he addressed him formally as Donaldson during the whole of the evening of their first meeting. Discharging in this way, as he thought, his duty towards good manners, he felt himself free to make such efforts as occurred to him to secure Jack's affection on his own account. We dined at the Savoy Hotel, and at the end of a (to me) inexpressibly tedious evening, standing straight on the street with the aid of the pillar of the door behind his back, while the doorman fetched us a taxi, and while Jack made a similar use of the opposite pillar, he wagged his forefinger unsteadily through the air.

"Well, Donaldson," he said, "it had never occurred to me that I should ever get drunk with any son-in-law of mine."

So ended the period of my youth—one of the silliest seasons, I think.

12

O N an afternoon in January 1935, a week or two before we were married, I found myself following Jack, who was dressed in a long, green, tweed overcoat of antiquated cut that had belonged to his father, through the dust and rubble of a building site round a large new building that had recently arisen in the suburb of Peckham. This building, which had been minutely planned to serve an entirely original purpose, had a front elevation of curved glass windows set in concrete two storeys high, and was functional, not in the architectural sense of the word in much use at that time, but in its response to the needs of an inspired conception. A few years later when Professor Gropius arrived in England he was to say that it was not merely the best new building that he had seen in England, but the only one that he found interesting. Although built with a flat roof and without decoration, it had an elegant buoyancy which was to remind one, when it was lit up at night, of a great liner at sea. On the afternoon when I first saw it, it was not quite finished, and it was for me the astonishingly material evidence of what seemed an incredible venture.

Later on the same afternoon we went to tea at a house in Gower Street. In a room, casually but characteristically furnished, which had a sparse air of asceticism and intellectual purpose, there were three men. One of these was Dr Scott Williamson, the mind behind both the building I had seen and the adventurous purpose it was to serve, the second a young doctor who was working with him, and the third one of a number of laymen who had backed and financed the undertaking. This was my first introduction to the group of people who were responsible for the experiment known as the Pioneer Health Centre at Peckham. Dr Pearse, the woman-doctor who worked closely in partnership with Dr Scott Williamson, and whose house this was, was not there.

This was also my first introduction to an entirely serious-minded and intellectually-sustained society, and I was confounded by finding myself unable to understand anything that was said. This was not so surprising, I afterwards found out, because they were discussing the mechanism of a key which was to serve the almost miraculous purpose of a calculating machine in giving access to the great building—one of the more romantic of Dr Scott Williamson's notions which never, in fact, materialised. It was true, nevertheless, that the every-day conversation of these people was on a plane and in a realm so new to me that, enthusiastically opinionated as I am, it was some months before I could easily take part in it.

This is not the place to discuss in detail either the aims or the achievements of the Peckham experiment. For those who do not know of it and for whom anything I write here may awaken curiosity there is an extensive literature. But, since in the years that followed this afternoon it was to be one of the two major influences in my life, I must give some explanation of what was both a research in human biology, and an experiment in medicine and sociology.

Probably the point of inspiration was when Dr Pearse, doing welfare work in London, found that the health of the populace was so devitalised that babies were being born deficient in health. "The youth of the nation is being threatened *before* it is born."* Clearly some means must be found of surveying the conditions that led to this devitalisation, and at the same time providing an environment in which the health of the parent might be built up. This led on to the belief that the unit of society that must be considered, both as a field of research and as the only hopeful sphere for medical endeavour, was the family. This in its turn led to the conception of a family club, where opportunities for social life would provide an incentive to families

* *The Case For Action* by Innes H. Pearse and G. Scott Williamson (Faber & Faber).

to join and an environment in which trained observation of the human material would be possible. In 1926, when a small house in Peckham was used as a preliminary experiment, the two rules which were the only condition of membership were, one, that only families as a whole might join, and two, that these must agree to a periodical medical overhaul.

Several years' work in this club convinced the two doctors that here was an unexampled field for the pursuit of preventive medicine, for research into the characteristics of health, and an ideal background for sociological work. They found themselves hampered, however, both in therapeutic work and for further advancement of knowledge by the small scale of their experiment. When they examined a child and found him ailing and feeble from lack of fresh air or exercise, they were unable in their small garden to place adequate remedial opportunities in his way. When a woman, suffering from the social isolation which appeared to be one of the great problems of life in the crowded streets of London, was found to be the source of a nervous tension which was affecting the health of every member of her family, the stimulus to activity which they could provide in their little house was often insufficient or insufficiently varied to attract her attention. They had failed in these cases both to remove the obvious conditions of ill-health and to create an environment in which it would be possible to observe the responses of ordinary people to opportunities placed in their way.

It was decided then to close the initial small-scale experiment and to devote the whole of their energies to an attempt to get the money and support necessary for a family club, large enough to be self-supporting by subscription once it was fully running, and in which there would be the complete medical equipment necessary for the periodic overhaul, as well as such apparatus as was considered essential to the complex needs of social life.

In their attempt to raise money for their venture they were surrounded by difficulties. In the first place the small group of people interested in this enterprise were not well placed to tap the sources of the enormous sums of money that were yearly given to charities. Quietly at work in their small backwater, they were not in touch with the vast world of charity balls, trust organisations, and ardent voluntary workers which was responsible for the raising of much of the money privately given. Secondly, their aims and ideals were too complex, and at this date too original, to be easily or attractively explained to the public. Thirdly, although in relation to the sums yearly given to hospitals their requirements for an experiment in preventive medicine were quite small, there was, nevertheless, to the untutored layman a breath-taking grandeur in their conception, a suspicion of reckless or extravagant planning, which could be overcome only by a complete understanding of the project and a faith in the ultimate viability of the method—neither of which were easily secured from members of the public.

If, therefore, one has to point to one single circumstance which would account for the fact that on that day in January I walked round an almost completed building, one can only record the un-exampled generosity of one young man who, having inherited the sum of £20,000 from his parents, transferred half this sum to the account of the Pioneer Health Centre. This imaginative action so stirred the group of people who witnessed it that they immediately subscribed a further £10,000 between them, although few of them were so rich that they could do this without unusual altruism.

When in this way enough money had been collected to pay for the cost of the building, it was decided to acquire a site and use the whole of the money in erecting the proposed Health Centre, in the belief that the building itself would both explain the intention and inspire the generosity necessary to fulfil it. On the day I visited it, I saw in the interior a swimming pool, one of the two largest in London, which filled the centre of the building throughout two floors; a theatre, a gymnasium and a children's nursery on the ground floor; dance halls, a cafeteria and rooms for such games as billiards, table tennis, or for such occasions as sewing parties or gramophone recitals, on the second floor; and a complete set of medical rooms, as well as a library (as yet unstocked) on the third floor. But in the Pioneer Health Centre's bank account there was only money enough to open the Centre and run it for one month.

It is sufficient to say here that, through the generosity of many private individuals, notable amongst them Lord Nuffield, the money was raised to keep the Centre open until it was closed because of the danger of air-raids at the beginning of the war; and that it was reopened again after the war, but finally closed two or three years later, because it had failed to become self-supporting, and in the changed conditions, both of the Health Services and of the availability of private money, it was impossible to finance. In retrospect, it must be regarded as an immense and magnificent failure, but as long as it remained open, it had many of the aspects of an inspired success.

The creative mind, as I have said, was that of Dr Scott Williamson. This is not the place to discuss the value or the quality of his work or his thought. That these may never now be assessed by their application to a living society does not invalidate them. The ways of mankind are governed by a hotchpotch of compromise and expediency which never certainly reveals or achieves the potential good. Certainly many of his ideas of that time have now become embodied in general sociological and medical theory and are truisms of everyday thought; and, in the memories of everyone who worked with him then, he remains a man of genius, a man with a brave and illuminating mind.

Into this world of serious endeavour, inexplicable faith, courage amounting almost to foolhardiness, I stepped that day in January out of the world of trivialities I had known, and was welcomed on terms of equality and intimacy because I was going to marry Jack. He had recently relinquished a job in Lloyd's Bank which had held, it was thought, considerable promise for his future, and he had now decided to take part in this experiment, which seemed to him to hold out much hope of interest and achievement. He was not exceptional, however, in making financial sacrifices so as to work at the Pioneer Health Centre. From the day of its inception until it was closed, it was always staffed by people of distinctive and distinguished ability who accepted very low salaries for the interest they found in their work there.

This, then, was the community in which much of the years of my early married life was spent. One thinks of it as a community, because, partly for convenience in their daily attendance at the building at Peckham where strange working hours were kept (2.30 in the afternoon until 10.30 at night), but partly because Scott Williamson chose to surround himself always with what might not inappropriately be termed his disciples, most of the staff of the Centre lived together in a large house on Bromley Common. And here, never tired of any of the aspects of their work, when not engaged at the Centre itself, they wrangled all day long. It would have been impossible for the mind of any young person thrown suddenly and intimately among them not to be influenced forever by their thought.

The most surprising to me of all Scott Williamson's characteristics was his lack of paternalism which, as far as this is humanly possible, was complete. He was not interested in how people should behave, or in how they might be made to behave, but only in how they did behave in any given circumstances. He was accused often, and I think one has to admit correctly, of lacking the scientific mind, because he could never be induced to conduct his experiment on the lines and with the method which other people thought necessary if its results were to have a wide-spread effect. But in his dealings with people he had an objectivity that was almost inhuman. And this made for a kind of democracy in the Centre which I doubt has ever been seen anywhere else. He used to walk about the social floors observing the members, and only where he noticed that some thread of behaviour was upsetting the pattern of natural response to opportunity of the mass of the people did he move to control it. He saw early, for instance, that people were not persuaded to attempt participation in a game or movement by demonstrations of skill, but rather made more shyly conscious of their own disability. He stopped then in the public rooms all the inevitable attempts to raise a side or a team for this or that game, and confined these enthusiasms to the smaller private rooms. In the larger rooms and on the main tables the fatuous and unskilled efforts of the amateurs led even the shyest people on to try their hand. He had a rooted objection to the leader in society, regarding him as someone who pushed around the human material he wished to study in spontaneous action, and who exerted the force of his personality to drive more ordinary people out of the true of their natural behaviour into activities unsuited to them and which they half-consciously disliked.

His unusual lack of the desire to improve or control put a strain on his staff that was at times unbearable. When the Centre was first opened, as is common with new ventures, it was in an unfinished state. Much of the equipment designed for the use of the children had not yet arrived, and in any case too little was yet known of the methods for their care and development in the Centre for any of the arrangements for their reception to have been carefully formulated. With the first member-families there arrived a horde of undisciplined children who used the whole building as they might have one vast London street. Screaming and running like hooligans through all the rooms, breaking equipment and furniture, they were not merely a source of despair to the staff, but such an offence to each of the new members (except individually to their own parents), that it seemed likely these might leave the Centre in disgust before the experiment was properly begun. In these circumstances it seemed natural to attempt disciplinary action, to make and enforce certain rules for their behaviour, and this would have quieted not merely the sense most people had that it was absolutely necessary to do so, but also the emotions they felt towards these noisome little beasts. Conspicuous amongst those who desired a release for their own aggression was myself. Scott Williamson would have none of it. He insisted that peace should be restored only by the response of the children to the variety of stimulus that was to be placed gradually in their way. When, in less than a year, he had reduced the chaos to an order in which groups of

160

children could daily be seen swimming, skating, riding bicycles, using the gymnasium or playing some game, occasionally even reading a book in the library, and where the running and screaming were things of the past, he gained an ascendancy over his staff that converted them forever to his principles.

These principles produced in the Centre what one of his staff was to describe as a "controlled anarchy."* And this in its turn produced an atmosphere, a lively orderliness, which was of its kind unique.

In his personal life he disregarded every ideal to which his work was devoted. His aim was health, but he had a natural liberalism which could not be restrained by rules. He himself seldom went out of doors, chain-smoked all day and was averse to the kind of moral attitude that makes people sit up straight or take fresh air. He was ironically disapproving when any of us tried to give up smoking, regarding this as an unhealthy and self-conscious priggishness to be teased out of us.

He was a strenuous talker. Quite often in the communal life he led he would start some conversation at breakfast and still be pursuing his thought in the early hours of the following morning. I do not think he conceived his creative ideas by clearing his mind in this way, or polished them against the minds of other people. I think these came to him in solitude, on some high plane he inhabited alone. But he was an inveterate and untiring searcher after truth, and he chose his companions for their ability to sustain this search through hours of conversation. Once, when he and Dr Pearse were staying with us, late at night Jack and I began to eat sweets.

"Look at our hosts," he remarked to Dr Pearse, "endeavouring to restore their energy by an injection of sugar into the blood-stream."

But he kept us out of our beds for an hour or two more.

He was concerned with the conditions of health or ill-health in all their forms, and he brought to bear on these subjects the force of his original mind. He had a flair for diagnosis, and a

* *Biologists in Search of Material*, by Innes H. Praise and G. Scott Williamson (Faber & Faber).

contempt for other people's opinions which led him often to cures of long-standing disorders or grave-seeming sudden illness that appeared little short of the miraculous. In the same way, he was never much influenced by contemporary medical fashion. He had, for instance, a great impatience with the kind of soft approach to psychological problems which was a feature of much thought and conversation at that time. Once a young woman who was very close to him, and who was thinking of marrying a man of whom he disapproved, consulted him about some behaviour of her beloved which had upset her.

"The man's a cad!" Scott Williamson snorted.

"That's not an explanation," this young woman said.

"It's a description," he replied shortly, "And that's all you need."

He was interested in every aspect of human behaviour, and he was entirely at ease with human beings. In the days when they were trying to raise money for Peckham, he could occasionally be seen with Dr Pearse at a cocktail party in a smart London drawing-room. Here, with his hair brushed a little better than usual, a Martini in his hand, he could be seen conducting the same kind of severely probing intellectual conversation that he had left behind him in the rooms from which he had just come. Nor did he ever find it necessary to discipline his thought or simplify his language for the members of the Centre. And so he was an extraordinarily educative power for people who came in contact with him.

When he desired relaxation from his normal mode of life, he read paper-backed thrillers with a concentration that removed him for long periods from the company which surrounded him. His rooms were always full of these books, picked up indiscriminately on the bookstalls, without regard either to author or subject.

He entertained constantly in the houses where he lived, but with a natural simplicity which wove his hospitality into the everyday sequence of his life, and one seldom went to his house without finding strangers there being treated as though they were members of his household, and made to converse with a concentrated attention which usually left them flushed with pride and exhaustion, but his devoted admirers. Dr Pearse, a person of powerful intellect and character, was, nevertheless, more nervous in society, and the difference in temperament of these two sometimes led to situations of especial joy to the rest of us. Once when I was at the Bromley house a stranger had arrived unexpectedly to tea, and Dr Pearse was fussing a little, apologising for the untidy squalor of the room, and for the lack of appropriate food, wondering whether the chair in which her guest sat was comfortable, or the light in his eyes too strong. Dr Scott Williamson said nothing, but to the initiated the signs of gathering impatience became obvious. Presently he leaned forward.

"Have some tea," he said to his guest. "it was made with putrid water."

He was almost entirely unpossessive. So little had he of this feeling, that he seldom distinguished in the communal society between his own belongings and other people's. Once, in the war, when the Peckham society were living in a flat at Hyde Park Mansions, after staying a night there I was leaving in the morning by train for Warwickshire. Dod, as we called him, fussed over me when I left, and insisted on giving me a large bar of chocolate in case I was hungry on the train. He could not have imagined that this would be necessary, because mine was a journey of two hours between breakfast and luncheon. I think he was touched by my loneliness, going off home alone in the middle of the war, and he wanted to show me affection. A week or two later I told this story (as an instance of his personal sweetness) to Mary Langman, who was living in the flat.

"Ah!" she remarked, "I wondered where my ration had gone."

He was a dictator; a benevolent, sweet-tempered, untyrannical dictator, but still a dictator. He refused at all times to act except in the light of his own vision, and he could not be moved to any form of compromise with the ideas of other people. The Pioneer Health

Centre was ostensibly governed by a committee composed of interested people who gave up much time to this work, amongst whom were those founder-members who had originally subscribed the money for the building. It seldom happened that this committee met without loud protests because they were being asked to ratify some decision that Dr Scott Williamson had already implemented, or to take note of the fact that a resolution unanimously passed at a previous meeting had already been broken. This was a body of intelligent and respected citizens, responsible to the members of the Centre and to the public. And yet they remained on and on, a committee of broken-spirited but voluntary guinea-pigs, because of their belief in the genius of this man.

There was another person of original thought on the staff of the Centre, and it was to her that Scott Williamson turned in the days when the children ran screaming and out of control through all the rooms. And she, pausing so long to take her bearings and digest her observations before she took any action that she drove the rest of us to despair, was finally responsible for the direction of the children in the Centre. She had a permanently ruminating mind, and she reminded me occasionally of my father; for, although he was a man of exceptional ignorance while she had a well-stocked brain, they both arrived at unexpected conclusions by their faculty for seeing life as though it had never been seen before. With Lucy Crocker, although this faculty served her well and enabled her to make new and valuable contributions to child welfare, it also occasionally led her into ludicrous assumptions, which were the delight of all her friends. Once, when she was staying with me in the country, she came in from the garden where she had been watching my small son, then aged about a year.

"I've been looking at Thomas," she said. "You know, when he was staying with us at Oakley, we could never induce him to move or respond to toys or apparatus we gave him, whereas here he is pulling himself up on the sides of that pen and completely engrossed in trying out new movements. Do you think it's because in his own home he feels a security that he didn't feel with us?"

"You don't suppose," I replied, "it could be because he's six months older?"

I never worked at the Health Centre myself. I have no natural inclination for that kind of work. Nor did I ever completely share in the absorption, the almost romantic idealism of the staff. When I first met them I suffered from a sense of my own inferiority, my natural commonplaceness in their society. They were on the whole too strong meat for me, and I was glad to escape at times into the greater triviality of life amongst more ordinary people. But I could stand them in very large doses, and, looking back, I think I owe more to their unorthodox thought, their freedom from the stereotyped views on which I had been nurtured, their relentless conversation, than to any other influence in my life.

13

IF the staff of the Pioneer Health Centre were collectively one of the two major influences on my life after 1935, they were probably also, by awakening intellectual curiosity, ultimately responsible for my response to the other. Jack and I became, during the years before the war, what is known as left-wing intellectuals.

The term left-wing intellectual, used originally to describe people of the educated upper classes who held Socialist views as opposed to members of the working class in whom it was more natural, suggests also a conversion to a point of view through the use of the intellect. The term covered a large range of opinion, of feeling and of people, from an advanced Liberalism through all shades of Socialism to Communism, from uneasy consciences in England to left-wing journalism in America, from schoolmasters and parsons to Harry Pollitt and Alger Hiss. The history of left-wing intellectualism suggests that it was to some extent a misnomer, that the conversion was often emotional.

In essence all conversion must be so. There may be a long period of preparation where the intellect alone appears to be involved, it may even be true that initially interest is awakened by an appeal to the intelligence, but the moment of transposition or of enlightenment, a moment which in retrospect can often be seen to have taken place at a particular period of time, in a particular place, as a result of a particular incident, is the moment at which the emotions ally themselves with the intellect to achieve a complete conversion to a faith, a philosophy, or simply to a point of view.

Left-wing intellectualism in those days was often referred to as a religion, and it did awake in many people an extreme ardency of spirit, so it may be permissible to refer here to conversions which those of religious faith must regard as taking place on a different and higher plane. I have often read the history of a moment of conversion to faith, where the writer was obviously struggling to describe a unique experience, and to share with his readers, if only in the smallest way, the circumstance of a visitation. On me these descriptions always fall with a flatness which I feel is attributable, not merely to the inadequacy of words, nor to the inconsequence of these moments of inspiration, but to the fact that I have not followed the writer in the intellectual and spiritual preparation he had made before he received the revelation. Nothing in his account of previous struggles with his conscience or in his mind has convinced me that here in like fashion in similar circumstance might go I. So that, when we reach the culminating point of the experience he is relating, I am always left with a feeling of bafflement; of incredulity, not at his response to a call which, if I am right in thinking it of a higher nature than anything I have experienced, I do not understand, but at the littleness of the human occasion which immediately preceded it. One can only assume that the whole of his nature has for a long time been drawn ineluctably towards this point at which his faculties, travelling before on parallel lines, converge together to achieve integration, and that the particular event which seems to precipitate this occurrence is almost irrelevant.

At those periods of history where there is no great principle at issue, it seems to me that almost all engaged political emotion is bad, in the sense that it is silly. One sees this best at times of a general election in England, when these emotions are struck to a violent activity which reduces the participants to a level of thought and behaviour reminiscent of a football crowd hurrahing on the side-lines. It seems to me that the only intelligent position for the ordinary member of the public is that of the floating voter, or, on occasion, that of the absentee voter. It is a trick of the politicians to pretend that abstention is feeble-minded, unpatriotic or undemocratic. If both parties are committed to a course of which large sections of the public disapprove (as they are at the moment in support of the manufacture and testing of the H-bomb), what method is open to us for registering this disapproval except that of an extreme apathy at the polls? In any case, as far as I myself am concerned, having deliberately engendered these football emotions on behalf of one party and one candidate once since the war, I found them in the aftermath extremely unattractive, and I decided, while maintaining an adherence no longer under my control to one of the two parties, to reserve my active aggression for moments when it is spontaneously provoked.

This was an easy decision for me, because I am not by nature interested in politics. For one thing I find it nearly impossible to read the newspapers, or to follow with any close attention events outside the orbit of my immediate preoccupations. This is not a fact of which I am proud. On the contrary, at least three times every year I make a new resolution to read at least one newspaper every day. But I can never succeed in doing it. Murders and treason-trials interest me only when they are written about afterwards by Dame Rebecca West or Mr Alan Moorehead, women's pages attract my attention only when I am thinking that moment of buying a dress, and debates in the House of Commons, which I mean to make my daily reading, somehow escape me, except when someone I know well is speaking on an important matter. I am interested in sport once a year during the Wimbledon fortnight, and each time I make afresh this resolution to become a newspaper-reader I find myself anxiously turning the pages of *The Times* in search of book-reviews or dramatic criticism, which always seems to exhaust my intention for that day. I attribute my complete lack of concentration to my initial lack of education in this or any other discipline of the mind, but I can only attribute the lack of the curiosity that should, without the need of concentration, inform me to a feeble and feminine temperament. It was a relief to me then to discover what seemed to be a higher motive for ceasing to take a very personal or deeply felt interest in politics.

There are, however, moments of history when the issues over

which politicians oppose each other are real issues, not of method, or expediency, but of the condition and future of the human race, issues which cause all but the cold-blooded to uphold one side or the other. Such was the period of the nineteen-thirties. Since it would have been natural to me, given my background and upbringing, to hold blindly and unreasoningly to one set of beliefs, it needed a conversion of the kind I have discussed, a conversion initiated in the intellect, but involving a change from one kind of emotion to another, for me to believe, as I did, that only in Socialism could any hope for humanity be found.

I owe, as so many other people do, the whole of the preparation for my conversion to Mr Victor Gollancz. But the moment of conversion, the igniting of the fuse, I feel now to have occurred at the time when I read an account of a working men's strike. I am in a difficulty about this. I have for years been convinced that what I read was an essay entitled "My Favourite Strike," and that it was written by George Orwell. But if this is so, it must have been written in some newspaper or journal, because it is gone without trace. And I hesitate to speak of it without finding some confirmation for my memory, because it happens to me again and again that events, of which I am so confident that I write of them as of things that are quite certain, and for the proof of which I only afterwards search, turn out never to have occurred, or, if they did occur, to have a shape which may even contradict my memory of them. So I can only say now that I think what happened to me was this. I read an article by George Orwell entitled "My Favourite Strike," and this described a strike for the right of the working man to get drunk when off duty. I cannot begin to explain why it should be so, and I do not expect to be better understood than I myself have understood the accounts of other people's conversions, but at the moment of reading those words I remember that I saw, or it might be more accurate to say felt, for the first time that the whole of the human race was composed of individuals in essence exactly like myself. And I felt, again for the first time, that it was insufferable that any of them should go hungry or cold, and, what seemed to mean more to me, that it was not enough they should be rescued from these conditions, since I could not conceive of life for myself, and therefore at this moment for them, in terms which did not allow for more than the simple satisfaction of physical needs. I was appalled by the horror, the boredom, the waste of many people's lives, as they appeared for the first time to my imagination.

The history of a person is, more than anything else, a history of development. This is not necessarily development towards the good, but when people regard themselves and review the history of their own development, they often do so with greater satisfaction than it is customary to admit. In literature as well as in conversation the middle-aged mood in which we recognise how little we have achieved, how jaded and morally unambitious we have become, is the one most often reflected; but I think that around the age of fifty the normal person in optimistic mood feels himself to be wiser, more courageous, intellectually more powerful, and more individual in the expression of his personality than he was in his youth, and it is this that enables him to bear the loss of enthusiasm, the lesser certainty about the importance of his undertakings, as well as the fading of those physical attributes which alone once seemed a sufficient contribution to life. But here my view may be coloured too much by my own experience. That is how I feel.

When I look back on my life, I do not count this beneficial development to myself. I see that, here and there, there have been strong outside influences without which I should have been a very different person; that if at a certain moment my life had taken a different turn, if I had married a different person, come into contact with a different society, suffered different experiences, I should not have been the same person I am today. But here, I must admit, I count my actual development for luck. I prefer the person I am to all those others I might have been. I apologise for the smugness which seems inseparable from the truth, and I am conscious that in this chapter there will probably be found something to annoy everyone. For many people it may seem that it is just those influences which I value in retrospect that have led me astray, just the thoughts I hold as a result of them that are most offensive. In any case, I am glad that in the nineteen-thirties my life was such that I read all the left-wing literature that Mr Gollancz poured from the press, and I am glad that in a moment of emotion I renounced one whole attitude to life and adopted another.

There has been so much written about the political feeling of that time, so many explanations, so many recantations, that I do not propose to discuss here in detail my experiences then. It is enough that they were similar to those of millions of other people, but not so extreme as to lead me into the Communist Party, and not so subjectively or neurotically inspired as to lead to a *volte-face* or to anarchic despair. There was an indignation then, and I am glad that I shared in it.

It is necessary, nevertheless, to discuss indignation, because it seems to me that anger and hatred are the mainsprings of all strong political feeling. One may adopt a point of view in good faith, the whole of one's reason and senses accepting it as the right and the truth, but the emotion that sustains a political belief, however initially altruistic, at boiling-point, so that it occupies over a long period the forefront of one's mind, is anger against the other side. I can remember now that my hatred of Mr Neville Chamberlain over those years was curiously little less than my hatred of Hitler.

I cannot any longer approve of this extravagant feeling towards Chamberlain, but I still prefer it to the alternative position which, given my class and background and the stirring events of those years, it seems likely that I should have taken up. I see now that much which I believed in then has proved to be wrong, many of the things that I worked for would, had they succeeded, have had a disastrous effect. (Russia, for instance, might have occupied Spain during the war and be there still. This, I think, cannot be helped. I have ceased to believe that it is possible to be right.

When one looks back on history, the wrongs and the rights of any side so often seem, in relation to the events they precipitated,

171

largely inconsequent and fortuitous, and (since one has an un-reflecting acceptance of the necessity for the world to have arrived at its present condition) to have a happy tendency to cancel out.

What seems important now is to decide whether the particular wrongs one supported were wrongs with which one can bear to have been associated. I can only say that I am glad that I did not think, as I might so easily have done, that the unemployed were largely unemployable; that accounts of concentration camps in Germany were grossly exaggerated; that Czecho-slovakia was a small far-off country; that any alternative method of government which attempted to deal with the misery in England would not work. I am glad I did not believe that nothing could be done to "level up" the living-conditions of the people of this country which would not succeed in so levelling down the upper standards as to destroy all art, all amenity, while producing a general squalid mediocrity, and I am glad that I did not care even if this last should be true. Again, I am glad that I do not spend my time nowadays in bellyaching about the level of income-tax and the lack of incentive.

Nevertheless, since the circumstances of my youth have left me today in what I regard as an intrinsically unintelligent situ-ation (that of a person who is politically committed in an age when the issues or lack of issues make the only intellectually tenable position that of the floating voter), I am bound to consider two other things. First, to what extent was the wrath that I felt in the thirties justified, and to what extent the satisfaction of a personal need? Second, to what extent is the partisan feeling I have now for the Labour Party a hangover from the anger of those days, and to what extent the result of genuine feeling?

There seems to be no doubt that some of the crusading fervour satisfied a need which is common to the youth of communities that are not strongly religious. There is a desire for ardency, because only this can assuage the desolation caused by the sense of the pointlessness of life which I have twice depicted in my own history. As life goes on, loves, responsibilities, resignation tether us down to the ground like captive balloons, but until the questing spirit is vanquished by the hold of life, it can be very painful. This pain is productive of very little, it seems, except for the same unanswerable questions, cynicism in one generation and angry young men in the next. Only where there is some true occasion for wrath and fervour does it often reveal itself in anything but gouts of self-pity.

In my youth there was, or so it seems to me, a real occasion. Nevertheless, there are so many examples from that time of men who were led by ardour to extreme positions which they have never since been able credibly to explain, and to views which they have since recanted, that I do not think it is possible for anyone to ignore the probability that there was some element in his own nature—absent in other people of equal opportunities, higher intelligence and moral character—which hastened the conversion and fired the spirit. In many people this element was the horror aroused by a first-hand knowledge of the misery in England, the unbelievable cruelty and suffering on the continent, and it is not surprising that some of them should have been driven over the edge of reason into the arms of the Communist Party. For myself, I believe that I had that natural predilection for a cause as a result of the boredom of upper-class life. All my life, surrounded by plenty and comfort, I had never found employment for an energetic intelligence and character, and it was this need that was supplied by the new-found belief that there might be other ways, greater hopes for mankind, and that this was a purpose to work for. And yet, even if this is so, I cannot regret it. I cannot regret any psychological weakness in myself—although here again I am sorry for the smugness because I know that it is exactly this faintly holier-than-thou attitude that sickens many reasonable people with Socialists—that released me from the intellectual blindness caused by the emotional conditioning of class and upbringing. The weakness of people of the middle and upper classes, and I am sure this is true because I have experienced it, is that they are prepared to accept the misery of millions of other people; they do not see any necessity

173

to break out of an insufferable situation at whatever cost to themselves, because they are unable to visualise the lives of these other people. When, at the outbreak of war, evacuee children from the slums of big cities wishing to go to the lavatory lifted their skirts and used the floors of their new homes, many people were far more shocked at the fact that an environment that could cause this existed in England than they were at the action of the children. But they had never before asked themselves the question, what does happen in districts where half-a-dozen houses are served by one outside lavatory?

When, however, one asks oneself the question today, why one remains emotionally committed to the Labour Party, it is more difficult to answer. There is the vested interest in one's past, the instinct not to question former beliefs by changing them now. With me this is strengthened by the fact that I live in the country. In country districts upper-class Socialists are still regarded by their neighbours with a kind of horrified bewilderment which might have been appropriate in the nineteen-twenties had a full-blooded Bolshevik suddenly taken up residence, and consequently are subject to a degree of misrepresentation that might not be believed in more civilised societies. Having suffered (not very much, because I do not care for the indiscriminate social life which is based on propinquity) what it is only a slight exaggeration to describe as social ostracism on account of my beliefs, it may be that sheer obstinacy has strengthened them. Certainly most of the changes in the structure of society for which I felt ardently before the war have come to pass, and a Tory Government has shown little inclination to reverse them. In my own party I am regarded as a faintly pale pink, scarcely off-white, Socialist, and I do not require more, to relax into political passivism, than reasonable standards of living for the mass of the people. And yet the Socialism which once took a virulent form has now become chronic in my nature.

I am told by people who have no incentive to gloss these facts that, with the left wing in power in the Conservative party and the right wing in power in the Labour Party, the differences in enlightment and ideals of the two sets of leaders are negligible, and in any case it is obvious to everyone that any party in power in England today is driven more by the facts of the world situation than by any pre-conceived ideology. Yet I have an emotional dislike of the Conservative Party which I think no circumstances could overcome. And this is of interest because I know that it is shared by many other people whose views are instinctive rather than analytical.

I think that the nearest I can get to the truth is this. All ordinary political adherence is governed by an unenlightened self-interest. And I find this more unattractive in the upper classes who have had the opportunity for enlightenment than in the working classes who certainly have not. It is not the leaders of the Conservative Party that I cannot stomach, but the large body of their supporters. The self-interest of the upper and middle classes demands the maintenance of the *status quo*, in as much as they fear any change for their own sakes. When one looks back on history, one cannot escape the fact that more cruelty and suffering have been caused by the maintenance of the *status quo* even than by religion. People of every generation, looking back on the last, are always shocked by the deeds of their ancestors, and naturally adopt the part of progressives. Only in the issues that affect themselves do they continue to use the same arguments, to shelter behind the same falsehoods against which reformers have had to fight throughout history. In any rational argument an intelligent Tory can deny that he is actuated by self-interest, can point to the progressive measures introduced by his party. It is in their off-guard moments that they continuously betray themselves. An example of this is the present Health Service in England. Tories can truthfully claim that this was conceived during a period when they were virtually in power. But a conception and the courage to put it into practice are two different things, and no Socialist who constantly dined out with members of the upper classes at the time of the inception of the Health Service is likely ever to forget the violence of the attacks, the chatter of wigs and of spectacles, the unkind contempt for the old ladies who wasted doctors' time in the surgeries, just as the old ladies of the upper classes had been wasting it for years.

In fact, the changes in the social structure that have taken place in England since the war may be due more to the trends of the day than to either of the political parties, and it is significant that many of these altered conditions can be seen in countries that have not experienced a Socialist Government. What is important to me is that, while these changes have been worked for and hoped for in the Socialist Party, they are a matter for continual bemoaning in the Tory Party, and, even if one allows for the English proclivity for grumbling and the fact that it is natural to oppose measures introduced by a Government one does not support, they are also the cause of a too violent initial hostility, followed by a deeply felt if half-conscious regret for our disgraceful past.

More important probably is this: just as one dislikes most in one's children the faults one knows they have inherited from oneself, so one dislikes most in other people the expression of instincts one disapproves of in oneself. It is necessary to me to think as I do, because I have the natural instincts of a member of the ruling classes. I fear and resent equality when I meet it. I have a tendency to do my shopping in our local town only in those shops where the shopkeeper has allowed the greater length of my bill to convince him of my greater worth in relation to the queue of customers awaiting service; my first reaction to the idea that the sons of people not rich enough to pay for it might form a large proportion of the boys educated at Eton springs from the same vulgar assumption of natural rights, of innate superiority, that I see reflected in the horror on the faces of even the most humane of my upper-class friends at the suggestion. I have little of the milk of human kindness, and I find it difficult to love my neighbours. Only the searing experience of the thirties saved me from an arrogant blindness, a deformedly closed mind.

14

AT the beginning of our married life we lived in a small cottage in Kent. For the first year we did not think much about war. After that, although we never really believed there would be a war, we lived with the fear of it always with us. In the cottage we were looked after by Mrs Saunders, the wife of the chauffeur next door, who came over a wall from her own cottage with the aid of two ladders. She had been a children's nurse before she married, and she had the highest ideas of the standards of privilege and service due to the people she chose to be employed by. Everything in the cottage was swept clean and polished, two cooked meals were served every day, people who came to stay were unpacked and packed for, my underclothes were washed and ironed every day. We both took all this for granted. If we had not, I doubt if she would have cared to continue to serve us.

Our lives had a curious rhythm, because Jack worked at the Centre which opened at 2.30 every afternoon and closed at 10.30 at night. He was at home every morning, but not again until midnight. He spent Sundays at home but worked every other Saturday on a rota with another member of the staff. Every morning we either went for a long walk or played golf. We were mad on golf just then, and on free days we used to motor to Cooden Beach to take lessons from Michael Bingham the professional. When we played together in the mornings we used to quarrel so fiercely that we often ended the round playing separately, one of us a hole behind the other. These quarrels arose because, although we knew from experience that it drove both of us to a fury, we could neither of us ever refrain from explaining exactly why the other had pulled or sliced the last shot.

I still rode sometimes, too, driving over to ride with Sam Marsh, and occasionally going out hunting. But after leaving Sussex I had had to take to riding astride, because unless one is very fit and rides every day a side-saddle is so terribly painful. I never acquired a strong enough seat astride, and nothing but balance separated me from the ground every time I jumped a fence. I had always forced my nerve a little further than it was good for, and riding astride I lost it completely. So soon I had not much enthusiasm for this sport.

In the winter we used to read a lot, and we had a big collection of gramophone records which Jack had acquired, many of them of classical music, but several hundred of them of what we called "hot jazz," but which nowadays rejoices in a variety of more intellectual titles. Most of the artists who are the great names of today were in our collection, not only Bix Beiderbecke, Duke Ellington, Louis Armstrong and Count Basie, but also Frank Teschemaker, and Mugsie Spanier, Red McKenzie and Stuff Smith, Jack Teagarden and Hoagy Carmichael, Buster Bailey and Fred Elizalde.

In the afternoons I sometimes went to Peckham with Jack, or sometimes I went to London, driving back in the evening to pick him up on the way home. Sometimes I stayed at home. We were very happy, but even in this first year of marriage I was harried by boredom. I used to wake in the mornings and wonder what I should do all day.

We did not intend to stay forever in the cottage, and we began soon after we were married to look for a larger house which we could buy or rent. Although neither of us was really country-bred, I having spent my youth in seaside towns and Jack his either in Cambridge or by the sea, we were both certain that we did not want to live in London. In that part of the country in which we were forced to live, so as to be near enough to Peckham, it was almost impossible to find a small house at a price we could afford. Houses seldom fell empty, and when they did, far richer people outbid each other for them. It was this that finally decided us to build a house.

Neither Jack nor I have much taste, nor even very strong

opinions on the visual arts, and we have always been conscious of this. We both, however, had a strong distaste for the contemporary habit of copying earlier styles of architecture. We were determined not to build in "stockbrokers' Georgian," or in any other pseudo-period style. We decided in an almost crusading spirit that the only intelligent thing was to build in the architectural style of our own day. The crusading spirit almost completely prevented me from asking myself whether I actually liked it. I assumed that I did, and, since I quickly acquired a vested interest in liking it, I have never known since how to answer questions that are put to me about the house that we built and lived in until the war. I think, however, that I very much prefer it to anything else we could have built at that time.

In the autumn of 1935 the great Professor Gropius of the Bauhaus was in England, a victim of the Nazi fervour against intellectuals and artists, although not a Jew. He built only two houses before, unable to find enough work here, he left England for America. One was a house in Church Street, London, the other the Wood House which he built for us. When we went first to see him we told him exactly what we wanted. We had little money but big ideas. We wanted a house with a double bedroom, dressing-room and bathroom for ourselves, a night and day nursery and two servants' bedrooms, with a second bathroom, a double and a single bedroom for guests, with a third bathroom, a cloakroom off the hall, and a fifth lavatory off the kitchen. However, the idea that the distinguished guests we hoped to have to stay might be woken in the morning by the little feet we meant to have pattering about our side of the house seemed to us intolerable, and we explained to Professor Gropius that the spare bedrooms and bathroom must occupy a separate wing of the house. We also explained that we liked sleeping out on summer nights, and the house should therefore have a loggia on the ground floor facing south, with above it a sleeping-porch, open altogether on one side. We also wanted a garage for two cars with an entrance directly into the house, so that on wet nights we need not go outside to get into the car. I give this list of our requirements, because Professor Gropius followed our instructions in detail, and this explains the possibly rather curious planning of the only country house he built in England. Later Mr Piers Thompson, the present owner of the house, after courteously asking our permission, built a wall across the front of the sleeping-porch on the upper storey, giving himself an extra room.

Professor Gropius built the house in wood because he liked to build in materials natural in the district, and in Kent these timbered houses are often seen. The wood that he chose was red cedar, at first the colour of chestnuts, but nowadays worn a dark brown, almost the colour of mahogany. He built it in two wings with flat roofs, sloping from the front to the back, with wide projecting eaves. Because the site that we finally chose was sloping, he designed a stone terrace in front of the house, one end of which was sheltered from the wind by a pretty curved glass screen on which we grew wistaria.

Nowadays Mr Piers Thompson receives much appreciation of his house, which to students of architecture is of great interest. Parties of American students, arriving in Kent with little time to spare and having to make a choice between Knole or the Wood House, have been known to choose the Wood House. But in our day, right from the beginning we were involved only and passionately in defence of it.

Most of our friends simply thought we had gone off our heads, while the Peckham people subjected the plans and finally the building to an earnest and meticulous criticism. When it was reported to us that it had been likened to the grandstand of a racecourse or nicknamed the "cow-barn," we were conscious of a certain vividness in the comparisons. Later, when the house was finished and we were living in it, Lady Cunard once spent the day with us there. She was very charming all day, smiling at me and murmuring *"Bonne cuisine"* after she had been given a disgusting irish stew for luncheon, and telling us all that she was doing for the new King in introducing him to amusing people, the Sitwells for instance, and Bertie Abdy. But the next day she telephoned to me. I had a duty, it seemed, to Jack and I was failing to fulfil it. I should see that he got a proper job and made himself some money.

"He is a very intelligent and cultivated young man," she said, "and he cannot spent the rest of his life looking after the poor and camping out."

Today, in our Gloucestershire farmhouse, we are subjected to a daily commentary on our taste in building. We have a splendid old countrywoman from the village who comes to do our housework. Every day she does the dusting with a care that involves picking up each object on the tables, and every day she leaves behind her a photograph of the Wood House carefully placed upside down.

But before the Wood House could be built we had to deal with more serious opposition. When we presented the plans to the local Council with an application for a building licence, they took advantage of a recent building law which was intended, not to prevent all experimental building, but to curb ribbon-development, to reject our plans and refuse us a licence. This meant that we had to appeal to the Ministry of Health, who then sent down an arbitrator to decide between us and the Council. For the purposes of this hearing we had a small model made of the house, so that everyone could see exactly what it would be like.

The hearing remains in our memories as one of those occasions of splendid jokes which all families have in their past, and which are possibly less hilarious to other people. The Council based their objections to our plans mainly on two things; that the house was to have a flat roof which was unknown and unsuitable in the district; and that this flat roof would present in their opinion a "strangely broken and uneven appearance."

Jack, appearing as his own counsel, called as a witness Peter Cazalet, a friend and neighbour, who was the owner of the land on which, if we won our case, we proposed to build. Hilarity was introduced because Peter was also the owner of Fairlawne, the great eighteenth-century house which was the pride of the neighbourhood, but which had from time to time received additions. When he appeared on the witness stand, there followed an exchange between Jack and him which was roughly as follows.

"Mr Cazalet, are you the owner of Fairlawne?"

"Yes."

"Has this house a flat roof?"

"Yes."

"Mr Cazalet, do you think it would be true to say that this roof presents a strangely broken and uneven appearance?"

"Well, yes. I think that it might be said that it does."

This was a demonstration of extreme loyalty on Peter's part, because he disliked the plans for our house as much as everybody else.

The second occasion for mirth was when the Clerk to the Council, pointing out on the model of the house the porch which had a flat roof, in miniature the same as the roof of the house, turned to Professor Gropius and said:

"Professor Gropius, can you really say that you *like* this feature of the house?"

And Professor Gropius, a little stunned by the whole proceedings, replied:

"Well, yes. I designed it."

The third took place after the hearing was over, when the arbitrator, accompanied by the Clerk to the Council and Jack, with two witnesses on either side, repaired to the site. Jack, passing out of the room in which the hearing had been held, said to Peter: "You come too," and the Clerk instantly objected that this would give Jack an extra witness. Peter, suddenly and icily changed from the character of amiable witness he had been presenting, said:

"When I require your permission to go on my own land, I'll ask you for it."

Before leaving this account of our adventure in building, I must also recount a story of our endeavours to acquire pictures to hang in the house. When it was nearly finished, there was an exhibition of pictures by Picasso in London. We could never in the ordinary way have afforded a picture by this artist, but when one is spending a large proportion of one's capital on one's home, it is an occasion for extravagance. Jack and I therefore went to the exhibition as potential buyers. But, although we were conscious of and depressed by our limitations, we could not care very much for the majority of the pictures in the exhibition. After some time spent there we found a small picture which was noticeably of the head of a woman, and which we were able to persuade ourselves that we liked. Before spending £250 on it, a large sum of money for us, we called in the only friend we had whom we regarded as a picture-expert, and asked his opinion.

"Look here," he said, in some despair, "this is not just the only bad picture in this exhibition, it may easily be the only bad picture Picasso has ever painted."

In view of the sum of money this picture must now be worth, irrespective of its merit, we regard this friend today almost in the light of a debtor.

In the early years of our marriage we felt that we were always in the minority, always having to explain our position, always on the losing side. Everywhere one went politics, or international politics, were discussed. In whatever society we found ourselves we were always alone in maintaining an opposition to the general view. This did not much affect our popularity in society. Left-wing politics were not taken seriously by the upper classes, never visualised as a practical possibility, or actively feared. Jack and I were regarded as relatively harmless eccentrics, sometimes as bores, at the very worst as "tiresome." It was not until the 1945 election brought success to our cause that some of our close friends found it impossible to meet us, while comparative strangers often regarded us with that faintly pleasurable horror with which, when we were children, my sisters and I thought of the old madwoman who stuck her feet out of the window, and with which one regards people who have incomprehensible vices. But, although no one seriously objected to our views, we were continuously involved in argument.

Jack has, in any case, a passion for argument, which never allows him to pass up an opportunity. Often we took part in violent disputes in which theoretically we were often victorious. This was because we had learned up our case with the thoroughness that was the Communist gift to left-wing thought of that time. Ever since I have been suspicious of argument which is too obviously prepared, too ready with an answer to every point. Lately I was given a book which was in the form of question and answer between Arnold Lunn and Ronald Knox on the doubts of the former about entering the Catholic Church, and although I had the honour of knowing Ronald Knox and know him to have been of exceptional goodness, the only emotion which this book inspired in me was one of shocked disapproval of his virtuosity, of the readiness and indisputable validity of his answers even to the most difficult questions. "Too much like the Communists," was my thought. But in those days the technique stood us in good stead.

Jack argues with a vigour that treats all men as his equals, and I spent a great deal of my time making him apologise to people to whom I felt he had been rude on the previous evening. Once seeing Colin Coote at a golf course, I forced Jack to go up to him.

"I feel," Jack said, "that I may have been rude to your wife last night at dinner, and if so I want to apologise."

"Not rude," Colin Coote replied. "Aggressive and wrong. But not rude."

And so most of the people we knew in this section of society took our views with patience and good humour. In other worlds we were constantly involved in correcting an impression that most of these very people were possessed of a Machiavellian intelligence and a conscious inhumanity, that they had foresight in fighting for themselves and a disregard for the sufferings of other people, all of which are inhuman. Christopher Sykes has described very well in his novel, *Dates and Parties*, people's bewildering belief that the politicians were capable of a long-sighted manipulation of events towards their own ends like chess-players. In this regard I was astonished when Claud Cockburn produced his autobiography to find the reviewers treating *The Week* as a serious contribution to that time. We used to take *The Week*, but I cannot remember ever believing a word of it. We used to treat the backstairs disclosures as a kind of spy story, a weekly melodrama which amused us, but on which we never placed any reliance. But the belief that the upper classes were composed of people quite different from oneself, quite without altruism, was widespread amongst liberal intellectuals of the middle classes. I remember that once we sent a young doctor from Peckham to see Oliver Stanley, who was interested in and helpful to the Centre. On his return he was exalted by his discoveries.

"He is the most extraordinary fellow," he said. "He believes in Prison Reform."

And so we spent much of our time, as we do to this day, defending those of our friends who did not happen to be present.

This did not hurt us very much. What was far more disturbing was acquaintance with some of the people we had to regard as on the same side as ourselves. Like millions of people, amongst whom, to their everlasting credit, were not included the leaders of the Labour Party, we believed in the Popular Front. This involved consorting with Communists. On two occasions when we met prominent and intelligent leaders of this party in England, whom we had from a distance respected, we were badly shaken by their lack of affection for, their unabashed manipulation of, the truth.

Nor was this all we had to bear. We were members of the Left Book Club, and we felt it our duty to attend meetings of the local group. These used to take place once a month in the house of a schoolmistress, and there the book of the month was discussed, first at length by a chosen member, and afterwards in general conversation. This is the kind of occasion which, in any case, I cannot bear. But here the boredom and idiocy of the proceedings were given an additional horror by the schoolmistress, who used to repeat at intervals of ten minutes and in tones of ghoulish relish: "But if there should be a *war* all this would happen immediately," war being understood to be the great breeding-ground for social revolution.

Lying awake afterwards in the sleeping-porch of the Wood House, and contemplating in fear and misery what war might mean to me, I used to think with hatred of this poor school-mistress.

We comforted ourselves with the thought that humanity is much the same all over the world, and that one cannot abandon a cause because of the people who support it. But we felt we where fighting helplessly on a losing side, with comrades who failed one continually, for a cause that could never succeed.

I never had much trouble over Russia. It always seemed quite clear to me that one should disown not support her. I regarded the Soviet Government as having appropriated words and a philosophy and, using them as a front for quite different activities, dishonoured them before the world; and I thought they were enemies of the cause of Socialism, not friends. But Jack, who is far more idealistic, was never able quite to relinquish his hope in Russia until, long after the signing of the pact with Germany, she attacked Finland. The arguments about Soviet Russia amongst groups of our left-wing friends were quite as heated as the political arguments we had with the Tories.

Amongst supporters of the Popular Front it was seriously believed that we should one day be involved in a *counter-attack* in our own country. I stress the word counter-attack because we never had any intention of attacking. But we seriously believed that, in the event of a Socialist Government ever coming to power in England by constitutional means, there was a danger that the erstwhile ruling class would attack it with force. When I look back on this ridiculous idea, the only excuse that I can find for it is that exactly this had happened in other European countries, and we were strongly under the influence of the left-wing journalists who reported from those places. Ours was a generation naturally pacifist, and we expended months of serious thought on what, in the event of internal warfare, the path of integrity would demand of us. After intense searching of the conscience and the heart, we decided for the barricades.

Over the civil war in Spain, I, less feeling than Jack, held strong belligerent views, but Jack exhausted himself on it. I suppose that, if it had not been for me and the children who were by now appearing, and also for Peckham in which he believed deeply, he would have gone to fight. As it was, he had to content himself with sending far more money than he could afford to the Republican armies.

Even over the question of the upbringing of my children, I found myself, amongst my friends, in an isolated position. I had fallen under the influence of the doctors at Peckham, who had decided views on this matter.

Since I first went to Peckham I had always been amused by the explanation of why this particular locality had been chosen for the experiment. The reply, most seriously given, was that the work they were trying to do was in itself so difficult that they had chosen a dormitory district, populated largely by employed artisans, so as to avoid the distractions of having to deal with members of either of the two problem classes, the very poor or the rich. By the time that I had my first baby I understood why, to them, the rich seemed almost ineducable.

The habits and customs of one's youth produce a conditioning of one's nature that cannot be dismissed, in the every-day use of the term, as merely conventional. In one sense I was completely conventional in those days, in my unquestioned belief in the necessity for myself of a certain number of domestic servants. As much as by my fear of war, the early years of my married life were spoiled by the continuing difficulty in acquiring these servants. When we moved to the Wood House we lost the invaluable Mrs Saunders, and we tried to replace her at first by a married couple and later by two women-servants, along with a nursemaid for the children. I was always in difficulties, and my mortification each time one set of servants gave notice with no others in sight was far greater than mere anxiety. In some way my whole pride was bound up in it, and I felt that the discourtesy to my guests and the demonstration of my own slovenly failure, should they not be waited on quietly and adequately when they came to see us, would be as great and as embarrassing as if I myself had appeared amongst them having just had all my teeth out. I had nothing to do all day. I did not reject the idea that I might cook or do housework myself. It never occurred to me.

(If it is wondered how I reconciled my Socialist views with my dependence on servants, the answer is that, because one is working for one kind of society, one does not cease to live in another, and if I had, on these grounds, considered doing without servants I might equally well have considered giving everything except the most minimum income away and living like the poor, an action which, and I have no shame in saying this, never entered my head, and which may be required of Christians but has never been required of Socialists.)

As a result of my conventional outlook, we always had poorly cooked food, we seriously overspent our income, and I, by nature intolerant, put up with more impudence then than ever before or since.

When it came to my children, however, I cannot put down my difficulties to the set of conventional ideas in my head, because these were all seriously challenged by the doctors at Peckham. I was very fond of the children and intensely proud of and pre-occupied by them, but I did not want to look after them myself, and I resented the time that I was finally convinced I must spend tied to their side by the requirements of natural feeding. The doctors had a horror of "nannies" (vindicated I think by the exceptional ease, friendliness and charm of the wartime genera-tions brought up without them), and a horror of the kind of life that was led by the children of the upper classes. They were very modern in their ideas of feeding and hygiene, and at war with the methods adopted by most of the nannies of my friends. They convinced me of my duty, and if I had had that complete absorp-tion in my family which I think is not merely attractive but possibly healthy in women, they might have made me like it. But they never could, and I loathed being here, as in so many other ways, in the position of a crank.

I compromised over the question of the nanny, by employing

young girls described in the advertising columns as Mother's Helps, who worked under my instruction and supervision. They were all awful; feckless and stupid, or rough with the children, irresponsible and always leaving. If they were of the domestic servant class, they walked out without notice, if they were of a higher class (as they sometimes were) they developed neurotic illnesses, rashes on their hands and arms or incurable headaches, which necessitated their leaving immediately to go under the care of their home doctor. Either way they added tormentingly to my already insuperable household cares.

Old Nan might have helped, but the scientific ideas of feeding, which she refused to obey, caused me to quarrel with her. She had been Jack's nanny when he was a child and, although in many ways she was the model of all the nannies of history and fiction, she was a person of such heavenly qualities that we can none of us ever forget or cease to regret her.

After Jack had grown too old for her, she never again took a full-time job. She used to relieve other nannies when they went on holiday and go to the assistance of households where there was illness or a sudden crisis. But she made a home for herself in Brighton with her sister and lived there when she was not on one of these temporary jobs. She had less than a saintly character because she had a genius for mischief-making which, although her intellect was so small that she was almost simple-minded, had the piercing accuracy of an X-ray in reaching the sore places of the mind. A household of servants, artlessly happy in their jobs and unthinkingly respectful of their employers on her arrival in a house, would, a few weeks later when she took her departure, be seething with suspicion, resentment and unhappiness. Infinitely more irritating and humiliating than this, although all the people who employed her regularly were forewarned against this characteristic, they too would be regarding their household in an entirely new light after she had been with them for a little while, so great was her talent for stirring the subconscious mind, for awakening the antagonisms latent in all of us. And, because this talent was instinctive and not calculating, it was no use reasoning with her or trying to threaten her into behaving differently.

Everyone put up with her because when she came into a house she brought love with her, and because her only demand in life was, entirely without the element of self-sacrifice or the self-defeating promptings of vanity, to serve other people. During the war, when I was alone at Gypsy Hall in Warwickshire and while she was still taking temporary jobs with other people, she used often to come to me straight from a household where she had had two nursemaids under her, and where meals were taken up to the nursery by a footman.

"This kitchen floor's filthy," she would remark as she entered the house, and within half-an-hour she would be down on her knees scrubbing it.

And although all her life she had been extremely haphazard in her ways, her darning and sewing a byword of lighthearted cobbling, and although for years she had reproved me for my fussiness, I turned her into a perfectionist when she was well over eighty, by refusing to let her do the cooking for me unless she did it as well as I did it myself.

I used to come into the house and find her waiting for me with the nervous anxiety of a writer who has submitted his newly finished work to his publisher.

"I've made the salad dressing," she would say, " and I hope it's all right because I did *exactly* the same as you do."

Right up to the time of her death at eighty-five she used to stay with us twice a year, and during that time she cooked and did the housework and turned out the cupboards and took down all the books and dusted behind them, doing all the jobs which no one else ever had time to do, albeit extremely inefficiently, though this was because of her character not because of her age. She died of a stroke which attacked her while she was blacking a stove in her own home. Even in death she was considerate. She might have had this stroke, and I often worried about it, while she was escorting the youngest of my children across England by train.

190

It may have been partly her natural disregard for perfection that made her so wonderful with children. She never worried them, never wished them to be cleverer or better behaved than they could be. She had a soothing power that left them, when she went away, impossible for other people to deal with, not because she had spoiled them so much, but because they were unused to the ordinary roughness of life.

But at the time that I first met her I quarrelled with her. She was already sixty-five then, very small, with a slight hump, but a beautiful face. She thought little of me in any case, because I had not been born in the right family, and she was damned if she was going to take any notice of the senseless ideas I had imbibed from the doctors at Peckham. I was young, filled with a hysterical nervousness about my firstborn which entirely destroyed my humour, and I banned her from the house. Looking back now over the years that I loved her, I am ashamed that I could not have managed better than this. But my action was quickly effective. When after about a year she returned to stay with us, we had taken each other's measure, and if I gave in to her when I could, she also obeyed to the letter any instruction about which she knew I was serious. Jack was her ewe-lamb, and she was prepared to go against her whole nature, while grumbling her views on the latest silliness under her breath, rather than be excluded from his household and the care of his children.

She was extremely robust and naturally unsympathetic. When one was ill she always believed one would feel much better if only one would get out of bed and make an effort. Entirely without self-pity herself, she disliked it extremely in other people. But she was easily won over by an exhibition of any of the virtues she understood. She grew to love me and almost to forget that I was not properly a member of the family, when she saw the work I did on the farm in Warwickshire in the war. She used to grumble that it was "no way for the children to grow up," and that the house was not "a gentleman's house," and that she was tired of hearing about "silly old cows," but she secretly adored it, and could not be kept away. She never let me know directly of

191

her approval. While she was with me she always compared my house disadvantageously to the homes of Jack's two sisters. It was only when one of them said to me: "I'm tired of being told how much better you do everything," that I realised that her natural caution and her fear of uppishness prohibited praise or direct displays of approval.

15

ALL the time the fear grew. It might have been more bearable
if it had been a real fear. But it was not, because, although
everything pointed to war and one talked as if one expected it,
one could not quite believe in it.

Once in London we met Lord Ashfield.

"Do you think there's going to be a war?" I asked him.

"Well, no," he replied. "You mustn't take any notice of anything I say, because my point of view is very silly. I just cannot
believe that in the end the world will ever do that again."

This was very comforting, because it was exactly how I felt.
But another time, when Jack had gone to London alone he came
back and said that he had met Knickerbocker, the American
correspondent.

"He said," Jack told me, "that nowadays he judges people's
knowledge of foreign affairs by whether they think there's going
to be a war or not. If they don't think there's going to be one, he
knows they know nothing about it."

That remark stayed with us for weeks.

The other thing that made the fear so unbearable was that one
did not know what to expect. Once Bob Laycock came to
luncheon. He had just been on a gas course and he said (or I
think he said, now it seems so unlikely) that one aeroplane over
Ascot could drop a bomb which would gas the whole of London.
Then someone had told us that orders had been given that, if
there was a war, and the dead bodies in London were too many
to be buried, they were to be put on barges and shipped down the
river; anything to get them out of the streets.

There was the other thought which came to one only in the
night. What if there was a war and the Germans won it?
What happened then?

We were beginning to have some idea, through the refugees that came out of Germany and the occupied countries. Jack and I had begun to believe we had a duty to do something for these people.

The first thing we did was not entirely altruistic. When one of our English maids left, we applied for a Czechoslovak girl to be sent over to take her place. But we looked forward to receiving this girl, whose photograph we had seen and who looked rather charming in a Slavonic way. While we were waiting for her to come, we wrote and assured her of a welcome, and she wrote back and seemed very excited at the prospect of coming to us.

When she arrived, she was stony with misery. She had genuinely looked forward to coming and had longed to escape the horror of her own country, but she had not realised that life for her was all that she had left behind at home. In England she was incapable of making any effort to live or to form new ties. She tried to do some housework in the mornings, but otherwise she sat all day long, looking blankly about her. She cried sometimes, but mostly she just sat in silence.

It was hateful for us. This was our home which we had just built, and in which we lived so happily together. It was horrible to think that for her it was a prison, a place she looked at with despair. So it was a great relief to me when I noticed the well-known nervous symptoms which had always preceded departure. She came out in a rash all over her hands and arms. I forget how she left us. I am sure she did not go to some other household, and I think she must have had such a complete breakdown that she was put into hospital. I only know that for years after this I occasionally heard from her. In her letters she always expressed gratitude and affection for us, and said that she wished so much she had not had to leave us. I do not think she meant this. I think that, as she began gradually to come back to life, she realised how coldly she had repelled our efforts to help her, and regretted it.

The second of our attempts was, in a different way, equally unsuccessful. One day when I had gone to the offices of the refugee-organisation to settle some point about this Czecho-slovak girl, I had been kept waiting in a large room half-filled with people. While I was waiting, a girl had come in and spoken in a language I did not understand, first to one person and then to another. She was extraordinarily beautiful, and when she spoke to these people her attitude seemed to be supplicating. Presently she burst into tears.

When I was finally called to the desk of the woman I wanted to see, I asked her:

"What's the matter with that girl? What does she want, and why is she crying?"

She explained to me that the girl had recently been helped to come over to England by people she knew who were looking after her, but the man to whom she was engaged had been left behind, and was probably in great danger. What she was asking was for the love of God to do something to help bring him over.

"Why can't it be done?" I asked.

The woman explained that now there was a rule that male refugees could come into England only if someone would put up £100 for each one, so that they should not arrive destitute and become the responsibility of the British Government.

When I went home at night, I explained to Jack that I had identified myself with this girl and him with her lover, and that we had better send the £100.

Soon after this we received a message from the girl herself, saying that she would like to meet us to thank us in person. So we asked her to come down for the day to the Wood House.

When she arrived she took from the start almost no notice of me, but on Jack she used openly and quite unabashed all those feminine charms she had in plenty. This did not annoy me, be-cause I could see that Jack was not much impressed, and in any case I knew that he prefers to make his own approaches in a matter of this kind. What made me feel so cold towards her was that her attitude completely ignored the fact that the person whose sensibilities had been touched by her plight and whose generosity had sent her the money was me, not Jack. She angered

Jack, however, because it quickly transpired that the reason she wanted to see us was not really to thank us, but to explain that when her fiancé arrived in England he would have to find work, and that she had been told that the only work he would be allowed to do was that of a domestic servant. This was quite impossible, she said. He was a person of great distinction and intelligence, a journalist, and he could not do that. Jack felt annoyed, because he believed, and who shall know if he was right, that in similar circumstances he would have been glad to do any work he could, with me as his partner. What finally completed our estrangement was our discovery that what she really hoped we would be able to do was somehow to help them both to get to America. In those days English people were not pleased to find that they and their country were regarded only as a convenient stepping-stone to America. Nowadays we are more used to it and do not mind so much.

This story had a curious end. There was some hitch, some delay in getting the young man over here, and before he could come war had been declared between England and Germany. And so he never came. Some time during the war I remembered our unused £100 and wrote to the organisation asking them to send it back. There followed some exchange of letters out of which I got no satisfaction, and presently I forgot the whole thing. In 1948 there arrived with the post on our breakfast table a cheque for £100—like an unexpected present.

We made one other attempt to help the refugees. A friend of ours, an English Jew who had many relations in Germany, asked us if we knew anyone who would put up his uncle and aunt, a pathetic old couple who were not fit to work, the man having been until recently in a concentration camp. We said that we would have them ourselves.

Dr and Mrs Mandelbaum arrived. They were intelligent and courteous, and, although they were a little dazed, they were not like Freda, the Czechoslovak girl, and they did everything they could to express their gratitude and to take an interest in our lives. Their manners were very correct, and every morning at

196

breakfast we would find them in the dining-room, standing waiting for us, although we had told them to help themselves and begin, and every morning they would both of them shake our hands, one after the other.

We were seriously anxious to help these old people and we were filled with pity for them. Dr Mandelbaum had been in Dachau and he told us that it was not too bad if you could manage not to draw attention to yourself.

"Sometimes," he said, "we had to stand in lines outside for twenty-four hours on end. It was all right for those who could manage to do this. But if anyone stumbled or fell from the cold or the fatigue, then the Nazi guards would fall upon him."

And he had explained that if you were old, the standing was made so much worse by the fear that your physique would fail you, and you would not be able to prevent yourself from falling.

And yet, in spite of all this, and although we are not naturally heartless, because every morning at breakfast these two shook our hands they began to be unendurable to us. After a few weeks we discussed it. We decided that Jack must tell them that every country has different customs, that we were unused to shaking hands in the morning, and that for some reason we would prefer not to do so. It is a small matter, he was to say, but now that you are in England you will want to do as the English do.

Jack did it very well, and it was all most successful. The Mandelbaums quite agreed that every country has different customs, and they thought that, if we were in Germany, there would be small things we did that they might not like. In any case they were only too anxious to learn to behave as the English. We went to bed much relieved.

Next morning when we went into the dining-room the Mandelbaums were waiting for us as usual, and courteously but firmly they shook us both by the hand.

They stayed with us, nevertheless, for how long I cannot remember, but until one day in the late August of 1939, when I said to Jack:

"I can't, I *can't* have the Mandelbaums. If there is going to be

197

a war, and you are going to go away, I can't have the Mandelbaums."

And:

"No," he replied, "I don't think you can."

And so he telephoned to our English friend, and said that he must make some other arrangement for his uncle and aunt, which he succeeded in doing without too much trouble.

At the time of Munich we sent our children with the Cazalet children to Flete, Lord Mildmay's house in Devonshire. And when Mr Chamberlain came home bringing "peace with honour," Jack took a great part in organising an open-air meeting in Sevenoaks, from which angry telegrams of reproof were sent to the Prime Minister. I was very glad he should do this, because I knew that it would not have the slightest effect. In those days I used often to look at the other women in the room when everyone was talking belligerently about war, and I wondered if they were really so intrepid as they seemed, and whether it was only I who was so craven. At the time of Munich, although I said nothing of this to anyone, I ceased to hate Mr Chamberlain for a little while and actually loved him, in spite of my shame at this feeling. I was always unnaturally quiet when the conversation turned on the necessity for war.

Some time during 1937 or 1938 Jack decided to leave Peckham. His work had been on the social floor, and, although he remained on as a director, he felt that, now the work was organised, it could be done by a great many other people, and held less interest for him. During the time he was looking for another job we suffered tremendously from anxiety. Jobs were so difficult to get. Finally he joined a road transport firm, of which Philip Dunn was chairman. This had unforeseen consequences. In the ordinary course of events Jack would have joined the Anti-Aircraft with Peter Cazalet and Anthony Mildmay, and if he had, I suppose he would have ended, as they did, in a tank in the Welsh Guards. But a recruiting officer came to the road transport firm asking for volunteers for a unit called Movement Control which was to run the transport in the war, and Jack joined it.

The hateful thing about Movement Control was that it was always sent abroad first and always came home last.

I cannot remember whether it was at the time of Munich or in the autumn of 1939 that we went on a Sunday to visit four friends who were staying in a house together. The two men of these families were both people of unusual distinction. One is today the Professor of a post-graduate course at one of the great universities of America, the other the head of the European branch of a world organisation. As we drove over to see them, we talked continually about the war, and we arrived at the house in a mood of fear and despondency. We were astonished to find that they were discussing with some glee the possibility that, if there was a war, there might be a moratorium on debts. They were both quite unable to make a living in peacetime England.

The other thing I remember very distinctly is the sinking of the submarine *Thetis*. For several days it was hoped that she might be saved or that there might be some survivors. All England thought and talked of nothing else, and everyone was appalled by imagining the men locked up under the sea. I think it was the last time in my life that the mass of people were able to feel a horrified and personal interest in the fate of a handful of men, however horrible the circumstances.

In the spring of 1939 Jack was severely reproved by one of his friends at dinner. He was told that he was becoming a bore because he was always so gloomy.

"You want to think things are bad," this friend said. "In the city they say that things are better than they have been for a long time. But your conversation would drive anyone to drink."

It was three days after this that Hitler's army marched into Prague.

All that summer the tension grew. We used to go for our holidays every summer to a house at East Runton which Jack owned jointly with his sisters. This year Jack left in the middle of the holiday to spend a fortnight with his army unit under canvas. On the night he left, Gilbert and Molly Debenham, who were sharing the house with us, and I drove him to Norwich to catch a train. On the way home we found that there was a practice black-out, and we had to drive by the light of our sidelights only. We found this impossible and highly dangerous, and we constantly turned on the headlamps. When we got home Gibby went to bed, but Molly and I decided to make tea. Then we decided to put whisky in the tea. Then we sat up half the night, getting quietly sozzled and trying to forget the camp and the black-out.

And the summer of 1939 hurried on until it reached the glorious sunshine of September.

16

ON September 1st in the evening Old Nan and I were trying to improve the black-out in the sitting-room of the Wood House. This was particularly difficult because the whole of one of the long sides of the room was glass.

I reviewed in my mind the events of the day. Jack had gone very early in the morning, and, as it was said that if there was a war his unit would be sent abroad immediately, I might never see him again.

Later in the morning, but still early, I had gone to the village school to help with the arrangements for receiving the evacuee children from London, who were expected that day. When I entered the schoolroom the loud-speaker of a wireless was blaring, and a man whom I did not know came up to me and said:

"Have you heard the news? The Germans are bombing Poland."

"Oh! but that can't be true," I replied. "That would mean war."

"It is true, I'm afraid," he said. "It's coming over the wireless all the time. If you listen you'll hear it."

Soon after that I heard it. The only conscious sensation I had then was one of physical shock, of the kind one receives after narrowly missing an accident in a motor car.

We waited about most of the day at the school for the children to arrive. We had been told that they would be very young children of both sexes, and everyone in the village had arranged to take one or two children of the sex most suitable to their own families, so as not to have difficulty with the sleeping arrangements. I had agreed to take two children (we already had a family of our own friends at the Wood House), and I had said that the sex did not matter so long as they both were the same. The bus that was to bring them seemed very much delayed, and we waited and waited.

Later in the afternoon the bus arrived, and out of it erupted thirty or forty youths who, to our astonished eyes, all seemed practically grown up. Something had been changed at the point of departure, and these boys were from a senior school devoted to scholars. Two of them were now in the nursery of the Wood House, and they were jolly and vulgar and noisy. They had already begun to stamp out their cigarettes on the nursery floor.

It was the thought of these two that started the wave of self-pity.

Presently Old Nan spoke.

"It's no use," she said, "to keep on crying."

I ignored her.

She pursued her thought.

"You cry much too easily. I was only saying to your mother the other day: 'The trouble with her is you spoilt her. The least thing goes wrong, she starts crying.'"

This was wonderfully untrue and unjust. But it was effective. For the first time for many days a flash of humour crossed my tired brain.

"Jack wouldn't cry," Old Nan went on. "When he was a little boy, he never cried. If something upset him, he just got under the table."

"You're quite wrong," I said. "When he was shaving this morning he cried all the time. But because of the ridiculous way you brought him up, he kept interrupting himself and saying: 'The damnable thing is I'm not even unhappy.'"

Old Nan did not believe a word of it. I watched her considering whether she should reply to it. But she had now reached the point of her discourse, and she passed up the opportunity.

"Well," she said firmly, "if it's going to be a long war, you're not going to be much use to the children if you just keep on crying."